WORLD
HISTORY SERIES ■■■

The Collapse of the Roman Republic

Titles in the World History Series

The Collapse
of the Roman
Republic

by
Don Nardo

Lucent Books, P.O. Box 289011, San Diego, CA 92198-9011

Library of Congress Cataloging-in-Publication Data

Nardo, Don, 1947–
    The collapse of the Roman Republic / Don Nardo.
        p.   cm. — (World history series)
    Includes bibliographical references and index.
    Summary: Focuses on the often chaotic events and larger-
than-life personalities of the fateful last republican century and
discusses the power struggles which gave way to a dictatorship.
    ISBN 1-56006-456-0 (alk. paper)
    1. Rome—History—Republic, 265–30 B.C.—Juvenile lit-
erature. [1. Rome—History—Republic, 265–30 B.C.] I. Title.
II. Series.
DG254.N37   1998
937'.02—dc21   97-10492
                                                              CIP
                                                              AC

Contents

Foreword

Each year on the first day of school, nearly every history teacher faces the task of explaining why his or her students should study history. One logical answer to this question is that exploring what happened in our past explains how the things we often take for granted—our customs, ideas, and institutions—came to be. As statesman and historian Winston Churchill put it, "Every nation or group of nations has its own tale to tell. Knowledge of the trials and struggles is necessary to all who would comprehend the problems, perils, challenges, and opportunities which confront us today." Thus, a study of history puts modern ideas and institutions in perspective. For example, though the founders of the United States were talented and creative thinkers, they clearly did not invent the concept of democracy. Instead, they adapted some democratic ideas that had originated in ancient Greece and with which the Romans, the British, and others had experimented. An exploration of these cultures, then, reveals their very real connection to us through institutions that continue to shape our daily lives.

Another reason often given for studying history is the idea that lessons exist in the past from which contemporary societies can benefit and learn. This idea, although controversial, has always been an intriguing one for historians. Those that agree that society can benefit from the past often quote philosopher George Santayana's famous statement, "Those who cannot remember the past are condemned to repeat it." Historians who ascribe to Santayana's philosophy believe that, for example, studying the events that led up to the major world wars or other significant historical events would allow society to chart a different and more favorable course in the future.

Just as difficult as convincing students to realize the importance of studying history is the search for useful and interesting supplementary materials that present historical events in a context that can be easily understood. The volumes in Lucent Books' World History Series attempt to present a broad, balanced, and penetrating view of the march of history. Ancient Egypt's important wars and rulers, for example, are presented against the rich and colorful backdrop of Egyptian religious, social, and cultural developments. The series engages the reader by enhancing historical events with these cultural contexts. For example, in *Ancient Greece*, the text covers the role of women in that society. Slavery is discussed in *The Roman Empire*, as well as how slaves earned their freedom. The numerous and varied aspects of everyday life in these and other societies are explored in each volume of the series. Additionally, the series covers the major political, cultural, and philosophical ideas as the torch of civilization is passed from ancient Mesopotamia and Egypt, through Greece, Rome, Medieval Europe, and other world cultures, to the modern day.

The material in the series is formatted in a thorough, precise, and organized manner. Each volume offers the reader a comprehensive and clearly written overview of an important historical event or period. The topic under discussion is placed in a broad historical context. For example, *The Italian Renaissance* begins with a discussion of the High Middle Ages and the loss of central control that allowed certain Italian cities to develop artistically. The book ends by looking forward to the Reformation and interpreting the societal changes that grew out of the Renaissance. Thus, students are not only involved in an historical era, but also enveloped by the events leading up to that era and the events following it.

One important and unique feature in the World History Series is the primary and secondary source quotations that richly supplement each volume. These quotes are useful in a number of ways. First, they allow students access to sources they would not normally be exposed to because of the difficulty and obscurity of the original source. The quotations range from interesting anecdotes to farsighted cultural perspectives and are drawn from historical witnesses both past and present. Second, the quotes demonstrate how and where historians themselves derive their information on the past as they strive to reach a consensus on historical events. Lastly, all of the quotes are footnoted, familiarizing students with the citation process and allowing them to verify quotes and/or look up the original source if the quote piques their interest.

Finally, the books in the World History Series provide a detailed launching point for further research. Each book contains a bibliography specifically geared toward student research. A second, annotated bibliography introduces students to all the sources the author consulted when compiling the book. A chronology of important dates gives students an overview, at a glance, of the topic covered. Where applicable, a glossary of terms is included.

In short, the series is designed not only to acquaint readers with the basics of history, but also to make them aware that their lives are a part of an ongoing human saga. Perhaps they will then come to the same realization as famed historian Arnold Toynbee. In his monumental work, *A Study of History,* he wrote about becoming aware of history flowing through him in a mighty current, and of his own life "welling like a wave in the flow of this vast tide."

Important Dates in the Collapse of the Roman Republic

B.C.
ca. 2000–1000
Latin-speaking tribes, including the Romans, descend from central Europe into Italy; by 1000, Roman villages exist on the seven low hills clustered near a bend in the Tiber River on the edge of the plain of Latium in western Italy.

753
Traditional date for the founding of Rome by the legendary king Romulus.

509
The Romans expel their Etruscan king and establish the Roman Republic, actually an oligarchy in which the people are permitted a measurable say in making laws and choosing leaders.

ca. 290
After aggressively expanding outward from the Latium plain for more than a century, the Romans complete their conquest of central Italy.

265
Having subdued the Greek cities dotting southern Italy, the Romans are masters of the whole Italian "boot" with the exception of the Po Valley in the far north.

264–241
Rome defeats the powerful trading city of Carthage in the devastating First Punic War.

167
Ptolemaic Egypt becomes a Roman vassal state, allowed to handle its own domestic affairs as long as it does Rome's bidding; having gained dominance over the large Greek kingdoms of the western Mediterranean as well, Rome enjoys nearly total control of the Mediterranean world.

90–87
Many of the Italian cities allied to Rome rebel in the so-called Social War; after much bloody fighting, Rome regains control of these allies, in the process conferring citizenship on all free adult males in Italy.

83
The powerful general Cornelius Sulla marches his army on Rome, seizes power, and makes himself dictator.

80
Ptolemy XII, father of Cleopatra VII, ascends the Egyptian throne.

ca. 60
Three powerful Romans—Julius Caesar, Gnaeus Pompey, and Marcus Crassus—form a political partnership later referred to as the First Triumvirate.

48
Caesar defeats his former colleague Pompey in Greece, then travels to Egypt and takes Cleopatra's side in a local civil war she is waging against her younger brother, Ptolemy XIII.

44
Caesar is assassinated by a group of disgruntled Roman senators; Octavian, Caesar's

great-nephew and adopted son, makes a bid for state power.

43

Octavian joins with his two main rivals, military generals Mark Antony and Marcus Lepidus, in a ruling alliance known as the Second Triumvirate; the triumvirs murder many of their opponents.

42

The triumvirs defeat Brutus and Cassius, the leaders of the conspiracy against Caesar, in two battles at Philippi, in northern Greece, virtually eliminating the possibility of reviving republican government in Rome.

41

Antony and Cleopatra become lovers and allies.

37

Antony abandons his wife, Octavia, Octavian's sister, for Cleopatra.

36

Octavian removes Lepidus from the triumvirate and places him under permanent house arrest.

34

Antony and Cleopatra stage the Donations of Alexandria, a lavish ceremony in which they illegally declare themselves rulers of the whole eastern sector of Rome's empire; most Romans denounce Antony as a traitor who has supposedly been bewitched and corrupted by Cleopatra.

31

Octavian and his chief commander, Marcus Agrippa, advance their army and navy on Greece, where Antony and Cleopatra are amassing their own forces; Agrippa captures the Greek port of Methone, cutting off part of Antony's supply lines; Antony and Cleopatra hastily move their forces to Actium, on Greece's western coast, where Octavian is already camped; Agrippa closes off the remainder of Antony's supply lines, trapping him in the region of Actium; on September 2, the opposing navies meet in a great battle in which Antony and Cleopatra are disastrously defeated.

30

Having pursued the lovers to Egypt, Octavian lands his forces near Alexandria; realizing their cause is lost, Antony and Cleopatra commit suicide.

27

The Roman Senate confers on Octavian the name of Augustus, "the great and exalted one"; Augustus also takes the title of *Imperator*, or "supreme commander," the term from which the word *emperor* later evolves; Augustus's ascendancy as absolute ruler marks the official end of the Roman Republic and beginning of the Roman Empire, which will dominate the Mediterranean world for over four centuries.

The Fall of the Republic in a Nutshell

Thousands of books and articles have been written about the decline and fall of the Roman Empire, the great political entity that existed officially from about 27 B.C. to A.D. 476 and for most of this period dominated the Mediterranean world. The cultural and political trends and events surrounding Rome's end certainly deserve such attention. Historians have long judged that the Empire's collapse signaled the transition from antiquity, or ancient times, to the medieval European world. That world not only preserved the best cultural ideas of the old Greek and Roman civilizations but also, over time, gave birth to the nations, traditions, leaders, and thinkers who largely shaped the modern world.

The Republic

The Empire's fall was not the first instance of a Roman world in collapse, however. Imperial Rome had been preceded by the Roman Republic, which had flourished for nearly five centuries after its establishment in 509 B.C. by the Roman patricians, the small but powerful group of aristocratic and wealthy landowners. Although all citizens of the Republic voted for some of their leaders and enjoyed certain civil rights under an impressive set of written laws, the patrician-controlled Senate wielded the real power. The story of how the early Romans, guided largely by the Senate, carved out the vast realm that the Empire eventually inherited after the Republic's collapse is dramatic and fascinating. At first little more than uncultured farmers, in the first two republican centuries the Romans expanded outward from their tiny homeland of Latium in central Italy and took possession of the whole Italian "boot." Then, inspired with the belief that they were meant to rule over others, in the next two centuries they conquered all of the lands ringing the Mediterranean; arrogantly, they came to call this great strategic waterway *mare nostrum*, "our sea."

Even more dramatic than the Republic's rise to power and glory was its relatively sudden decline and fall in its fifth and final century. This book focuses on the often chaotic events and larger-than-life personalities of this fateful last republican century. As classical scholar Michael Crawford points out, these events and characters brought about a cataclysm, or violent upheaval, nearly as great as that which would later engulf the Empire:

"A century like that between 133 B.C. and 31 B.C., which killed perhaps 200,000 men in 91–82 and perhaps 100,000 men in 49–42, and which destroyed a system of government after 450 years *was* a cataclysm."[1]

Class Division and Greed

Historians have suggested many reasons for the Republic's decline and ultimate collapse. Some point to an ever-widening gap between rich upper-class Romans and the much more numerous members of the poor lower classes. According to noted historian Chester G. Starr, "As the rich and poor drew further apart, the lower classes lent an attentive ear to demagogues [leaders who appealed to the emotions of the populace] who promised to elevate them or at least to destroy the ever-more-vicious mastery of the wrangling senatorial order."[2] Distrust inherent between social classes made it easier for popular leaders to play one class against another and thereby to foster civil strife. A series of savage and horrendously destructive civil wars did, after all, contribute heavily to the Republic's decline and final breakdown.

At the same time, the Republic suffered because of increasing divisiveness, as well as increasing greed and selfishness, within the upper classes themselves. This was a particularly alarming trend, for traditionally many of these upper-class men

The opulence in which members of the privileged Roman senatorial class lived is illustrated in this drawing of an upper-class Roman house, or domus. *The garden, or* peristylum, *is visible beyond the arch.*

controlled the Senate, which exercised a guiding influence over not only the government but literary, cultural, and state religious affairs, as well. As Starr comments, when this elite could no longer rule efficiently, both the state and traditional society were, in a very real sense, doomed.

[The] aristocrats were interested primarily in the heaping up of wealth, in living luxuriously, and in gaining political power. Serious attention to the problems of empire is rarely to be found, and the nobles were more at-

A bust of Augustus Caesar. After decades of intermittent and devastating civil wars, he overhauled the republican government to form the autocratic Empire.

tracted by the amenities of life than by the essentials of civilization. Even more dangerous was the fact that the unity of the upper classes was rapidly dissolving. Roman nobles had long been proud of their individual dignity and had fiercely vied for the outward marks of dignity, which in their eyes were the great offices of state. . . . As the nobles grew richer . . . family life tended to dissolve, the prosecution of noble feuds became ever more vicious. . . . It became increasingly doubtful whether the weak Roman form of government [i.e., the oligarchy of upper-class senators and the officials they controlled] could preserve individual initiative in the political sense and also continue to govern the Mediterranean world. The ruthless effort of each Roman noble to rise by pushing down his peers had historically to lead to the destruction of the state . . . the domination of Rome by one man and . . . the destruction of political liberty for all.[3]

Indeed, the inability of republican government to contain the greed and ambitions of its own leaders while trying to rule the vast Roman realm did inevitably lead to one-man rule—namely the Empire, lorded over by a long line of emperors beginning with Augustus Caesar in 27 B.C.

The Clash of the Powerful

Overriding the growing divisions between the rich and poor classes and within the ruling upper classes was the increasing exploitation of these divisions by powerful, hugely ambitious individuals seeking personal gain. This volume takes the position that the power struggles of political and military strongmen, including Marius, Sulla, Caesar, Pompey, Antony, and finally Octavian, who, renamed Augustus, effected the transition from Republic to Empire, were the chief cause of the Republic's demise.[4] Further, what made it possible for these men to run roughshod over the state was a glaring defect of republican government itself. There simply were no established strong institutional controls and safeguards to maintain order and keep power-hungry army generals from running amok. As Crawford puts it:

> The struggles between politicians during the Republic were given free rein by the failure to develop communal institutions for the maintenance of order; thus, even legal procedure often involved the use of an element of self-help, as in bringing a defendant to court [the plaintiff was obliged to do so because the state did not provide police to round up accused criminals]. Such a state of affairs perhaps did not matter greatly in a small rural community [as Rome had been before its rise to world power]. . . . But when men turned to force in the late Republic to resolve political differences, the result was catastrophic, with armies composed of many legions [large military regiments] rapidly involved.[5]

The Republic had long been ruled by a small group of individuals. As long as they had managed to work together for the good of the state, that state had thrived. But when those individuals repeatedly faced off, with large armies to back them up, they inevitably crushed the state underfoot. That, in a nutshell, is the unfortunate story of the fall of the Roman Republic. What follows are the dramatic and often gory details.

1 An Appetite for War: The Growth of Roman Imperialism

The terrible civil wars that climaxed in the fall of the Roman Republic in the last decades of the first century B.C. were motivated mainly by the desperate desire for power. A series of ambitious individuals sought complete military and political dominance over the huge Mediterranean empire Rome had acquired in the preceding few centuries. This great expanse of territory stretched from Spain in the west to Asia Minor, what is now Turkey, in the east; the empire also encompassed large sections of northern Africa and much of Gaul, what is now France and Belgium.

That all of these lands had been won by conquest indicates that the leading combatants of the civil wars—Caesar, Antony, Octavian, and others—were hardly unique in their liberal use of brute military force to gain power. Indeed, imperialism, a nation's expansion of power and influence through its domination of other nations, had long been the central tenet of Roman foreign policy. From their earliest years, the Romans had showed themselves to be eminently practical, resourceful, and resilient as a people. But they also developed a highly arrogant attitude, believing that their own ways and ideas were superior and therefore that they were destined to rule over others. No Roman writer captured this conceited view more elegantly than the poet Ovid, who was born in the Republic's waning years. "Even as I speak I see our destiny," he wrote, "the city of our sons and sons of sons, greater than any city we have known, or has been known or shall be known to men."[6]

For the Romans, there was no question about how that special destiny must be obtained; to them, as it was to all other ancient peoples, naked force was the most natural and expected method of getting ahead. As the late classical scholar Dorothy Mills pointed out:

> There was one great difference between ancient and modern times. One of the greatest problems that the world today is trying to solve is how great and powerful nations can live side by side in peace and friendship. The ancient world had not discovered that such a state of affairs was even possible. To the statesmen and thinkers of those days it seemed natural and right that one great and powerful state should have dominion over those that were weaker. . . . One must rule, the others obey, and such a question could only be settled by war.[7]

A review of the main events of Roman history leading up to the Republic's fateful final century clearly reveals how Rome, in

An artist's conception of the ancient Italian city of Veii, the principal stronghold of the Etruscans, whose culture strongly influenced the early Romans.

an ever-widening spiral of aggression and expansion, consistently applied this maxim of the strong dominating the weak.

From Rustic Farmers to Resourceful Republicans

The early Romans evolved from one of a group of Latin-speaking tribes that descended from central Europe into Italy beginning about 2000 B.C. By about 1000, the Romans had established villages on seven low hills at a bend in the Tiber River on the northern edge of the fertile plain of Latium. This plain was bordered in the west by the Mediterranean Sea and in the east by the rugged Apennines, the mountain chain running north-south through the Italian boot. One of the seven hills, the Palatine, may have been the original site of what would later become the most powerful city in the world. According to historian Donald R. Dudley:

> Ancient legend and modern archaeology converge in the story of the Palatine Hill in Rome. On this hill, on the 21st [of] April in the year later agreed upon [by Roman scholars] to have been 753 B.C., tradition asserts that Romulus [perhaps an early king] founded with due ritual the city of Rome. . . . Archaeology confirms the settlement of a pastoral community on the Palatine Hill sometime about 750 B.C. . . . But they were not the only . . . settlers on the site. Other such villages are known on the Esquiline and Quirinal [and other neighboring hills]. At some date we cannot determine these scattered communities coalesced [came together] into a larger unit, to which for the first time the name of Rome may be given.[8]

At first, the Romans were rustic, uncultured farmers and shepherds who lived in timber shacks with thatched roofs. They early came under the sway of a more advanced people, the Etruscans, who inhabited the plains north of Latium, a region then known as Etruria.[9] But it did not take long for the Romans to show their tough-minded, resourceful, and aggressive tendencies. Sick of Etruscan rule, in about 509 the city's leading citizens boldly expelled their Etruscan king, Tarquinius Superbus, and established the Roman Republic.

Rome's new republican government, based to some small extent on the democracy that was then growing in Athens, a prominent city-state in Greece, was run by representatives of the people. But Roman leaders at first defined "the people" rather narrowly. Only free adult males who owned weapons (and were therefore eligible for military service), a group that

The Founding of Rome

According to Rome's most popular legend, the city was established in 753 B.C. by a young man named Romulus shortly after the death of his brother Remus. This excerpt from the first-century A.D. Greek historian Plutarch's Life of Romulus *(from his famous* Lives*) describes how the initial foundations of the city were supposedly laid.*

"Romulus, having buried his brother Remus . . . set to building his city; and sent for men out of Tuscany [then Etruria, homeland of the Etruscans], who directed him . . . in all the ceremonies to be observed, as in a religious rite. First, they dug a round trench . . . and into it solemnly threw the first-fruits of all things either good by custom or necessary by nature; lastly, every man taking a small piece of earth of the country from whence he came, they all threw [the piece] in randomly together. Making this trench . . . their center, they laid out the boundary of the city in a circle round it. Then the founder [Romulus] fitted to a plow a metal plowshare [blade], and, yoking together a bull and a cow, drove himself a deep line or furrow round the boundary. . . . With this line they laid out the [city] wall; and where they designed to make a gate, there they . . . left a space. . . . As for the day they began to build the city, it is universally agreed to have been the twenty-first of April, and that day the Romans annually keep holy, calling it their country's birthday. At first, they say, they sacrificed [to the gods] no living creature on this day, thinking it fit to preserve the feast of their country's birthday pure and without stain of blood."

Romulus, founder of Rome.

made up a minority of the population, could vote or hold public office. Some of these citizens met periodically in a body called the Assembly, which proposed and voted on new laws and also annually elected two consuls, or administrator-generals, to run the state and lead the army. A second legislative body, the Senate, was composed exclusively of well-to-do patricians, who held their positions for life. Although in theory the senators were mere governmental advisers, in reality they usually dictated policy to the consuls and, through the use of wealth and high position, indirectly influenced the way the members of the Assembly voted. Thus, the Senate held the real power in Rome, making the Republic an oligarchy rather than a true democracy like Athens.

A Genius for Political Organization

Yet in an age when kings and other absolute monarchs ruled almost everywhere else in the known world, the Roman Republic was a very progressive and enlightened political entity indeed. Though most Romans did not have a say in state policy, many had a measurable voice in choosing leaders and making laws, a number of which offered an umbrella of protection for members of all classes against the arbitrary abuses of potentially corrupt leaders. "Law is the bond which secures these our privileges in the commonwealth [empire]," the republican champion Marcus Tullius Cicero would later write, "the foundation of our . . . liberty, the fountainhead [main source] of justice. Within the law are reposed the mind and heart, the judgment

and conviction of the state." [10] For these and other reasons, republican government proved increasingly flexible and largely met the needs of Romans of all classes.

As a result, the people came to view their system with intense pride and patriotism, feelings that fueled the first stages of Roman expansion. To many Romans, the success of their republican system was no chance event, but rather ordained by the gods, who, it was thought, favored Rome above all other cities. This same spirit would motivate the poet Virgil in the fateful first century B.C.; in his epic *Aeneid* the great god Jupiter says that for the Romans "I see no measure nor date [and] I grant them dominion without end . . . the master-race, the wearers of the Toga." [11] This belief in a greater destiny inspired the Romans to channel their aggressive tendencies in a new direction—outward. In the fifth century B.C., Roman armies began marching outward from Latium and subduing neighboring peoples. Among those who fell under Rome's control were its former rulers, the Etruscans, as well as many powerful and well-organized hill tribes, including the warlike Samnites of south-central Italy.

Much of the success of the Romans' early conquests was the result of their genius for political organization. Instead of ruling conquered peoples with an iron fist, they took the wiser and more fruitful approach of cultural assimilation. They introduced to such peoples the Latin language, as well as Roman ideas, laws, and customs. In addition to this "Romanization" process, Rome forged long-lasting alliances with many of its former enemies. "What made the Romans so remarkable," comments the prolific classical scholar Michael Grant,

A view from one wing of the Senate house, where the Romans debated and decided on important affairs of state.

such agreements was extended across the whole of central Italy.[12]

This rather lenient and very efficient method of administration did more than make it easier for Rome to control conquered lands. It also instilled in the inhabitants of the absorbed territories some degree of gratitude and eventually a sense of pride and patriotism in Rome and the Roman system. Thus, the Romans successfully solidified their gains partly by fostering among their former adversaries feelings of loyalty toward Rome. Cicero later wrote:

> Every citizen of a corporate town [one annexed by Rome] has, I take it, two fatherlands, that of which he is a native, and that of which he is a citizen. I will never deny my allegiance to my native town, only I will never forget that Rome is my greater Fatherland, and that my native town is but a portion of Rome.[13]

Perhaps the key element fostering such allegiance to Rome among the conquered peoples was citizenship, granted so that they might feel they had truly become part of the Roman commonwealth. As will be seen, in later years the republican government would become lax in granting such citizenship, a mistake that Rome would pay for in blood.

Roman Daring and Determination

was a talent for patient political reasonableness that was unique in the ancient world. . . . On the whole, Rome found it advisable . . . to keep its bargains with its allies, displaying a self-restraint, a readiness to compromise, and a calculated generosity that the world had never seen. And so the allies, too, had little temptation to feel misused. The proud Samnites, it is true, had lost a considerable amount of their land to Roman settlers. . . . But they were only a few out of a grand total of one hundred and twenty Italian communities with which Rome, in due course, formed perpetual alliances. After the end of the Samnite wars [about 290 B.C.] a network of

Gaining control of central Italy, rather than satisfying Rome's appetite for territory and power, only stoked the coals of its growing imperialism. In the late 280s B.C.

the Romans turned on the numerous Greek cities that had sprung up across southern Italy in the preceding few centuries. Some of these cities were larger and all were more culturally advanced and splendid than Rome, which was still a relatively small, dirty, and uncultured community. But the Italian Greeks were disunited and their armies could not match the size and caliber of those fielded by Rome.[14] By 265, the Romans had absorbed the Greek lands and become the undisputed masters of all Italy south of the Po Valley, the northern region bordering the towering barrier of the Alps mountain range.

Having emerged as one of the strongest Mediterranean powers, Rome next cast its gaze beyond the shores of Italy and onto the coasts of the sea's western sphere. At the time, this region was largely

The Republic's Highest Officers

The famous first-century B.C. republican senator, orator, and writer Cicero described some of the Republic's highest public offices, including those of aedile, censor, praetor, consul, and dictator, in this excerpt from his Laws *(quoted in Lewis and Reinhold's* Roman Civilization*).*

"There shall also be aediles, who shall be caretakers of the city, of the markets, and of the traditional games. . . . Censors shall make a list of the citizens, recording their ages, families, and slaves and other property. They shall have charge of the temples, streets, and aqueducts within the city, and of the public treasury and the revenues. . . . They shall enroll the recruits for the cavalry and infantry. . . . They shall regulate the morals of the people; they shall allow no one guilty of dishonorable conduct to remain in the Senate. They shall be two in number and hold office for five years. . . . The administrator of justice, who shall decide or direct the decision of civil cases, shall be called praetor; he shall be the guardian of the civil law. There shall be as many praetors, with equal powers, as the Senate shall decree or the people command. There shall be two magistrates with royal powers. Since they precede, judge, and consult, they shall be called . . . consuls. In the field [of battle] they shall hold the supreme military power and be subject to no one. The safety of the people shall be their highest law. . . . But when a serious war or civil dissensions arise, one man [a dictator] shall hold, for not longer than six months, the power which ordinarily belongs to the two consuls. . . . And after being appointed under favorable auspices, he shall be master of the people."

controlled by Carthage, a powerful trading city located at the northern tip of Tunisia, on the African coast. From 264 to 241, Rome and Carthage grappled in what proved to be the most devastating war fought anywhere in the world up to that time. Rome won this so-called First Punic War, in large degree because it took the bold step of building its first fleet of warships.[15] This was a classic demonstration of the Romans' renowned practicality, resourcefulness, and determination. According to the second-century B.C. Greek historian Polybius, the building of some 140 ships in only sixty days shows

> better than anything else how spirited and daring the Romans are when they are determined to do a thing. It was not that they had fairly good resources for it, but they had none whatever, nor had they ever given a thought to the sea; yet when they once had conceived the project they took it in hand so boldly, that before gaining any experience in the matter they at once engaged [challenged] the Carthaginians, who had held for generations undisputed command of the sea.[16]

Rome's new naval power gained it the main prize of the First Punic War—the large island of Sicily, at the tip of the Italian boot. Control of this rich and fertile island, along with the potential of the Romans' mighty war fleets, seemed only to confirm their belief in a greater destiny. Thereafter, Rome was thoroughly committed to the policy of foreign imperialism. As historian James Henry Breasted explains:

> For the first time she held territory outside of Italy, and from this step she was never able to withdraw. It has been compared with the action of the United States in taking Puerto Rico and the Philippines; for in gaining interests and responsibilities across the sea a nation is at once thrown into conflict with other powers having similar interests, and this conflict of interests never reaches an end, but easily and usually leads from one war to another.[17]

And so it was with Rome. It fought and won two more bloody wars with Carthage, which gave it vast new territories, including Spain, the western Mediterranean islands, and much of northern Africa.

The Roman Lake

Next, the Romans turned eastward and attacked the Greek kingdoms clustered in the sea's eastern sphere. The first of these kingdoms to fall to Rome was Macedonia, consisting mainly of Greece and parts of Asia Minor. Macedonia's king, Philip V, had allied himself with Carthage during the Second Punic War (218–202 B.C.); two years after their victory in that stupendous conflict the Romans were ready to punish the Greeks.

The three-year-long so-called Second Macedonian War was noteworthy because it pitted the Mediterranean world's two most prestigious and feared military systems against each other. The Greeks employed a unique battle formation known as the Macedonian phalanx. This consisted of thousands of soldiers arrayed in ranks, one behind the other, each man wielding a long spear, or battle pike. The men in each rearward rank held increasingly longer pikes, so that the tips projected out-

This painting depicts the Romans besieging Carthage in 146 B.C., in the climax of the Third Punic War. The siege culminated in six days of savage and bloody house-to-house fighting.

ward from the front of the formation, creating an impenetrable and frightening mass of spearpoints that resembled a giant porcupine with its quills erect. When the mighty phalanx marched forward, it usually demolished all before it.

By contrast, early Roman armies consisted of legions, groups of about 4,500 to 5,000 soldiers. On the battlefield, each legion broke down into smaller units, called maniples, of 60 to 120 men each, which could be moved to various positions for tactical advantage. For example, sometimes the maniples were arranged in a checkerboard pattern; at other times they formed huge diagonal lines, wedges, and so on. An individual maniple or group of maniples was less formidable than a large Greek phalanx. But the Roman units could move back, forward, and around quickly at a commander's order, giving the Roman army a degree of flexibility that the stiff, monolithic phalanx lacked.

The final, decisive battle of the Second Macedonian War, fought in 197 B.C. at Cynoscephalae, in Thessaly in central Greece, showed that the Greek system, which had largely dominated

Mediterranean land warfare for over a century, had become outmoded. Historian John Warry describes the battle:

> The uneven ground seriously hindered the Macedonian phalanx, but heavy mist earlier in the day also hampered Roman mobile tactics. On both sides the right wing was victorious, but the scales were tipped in Rome's favor by a tribune [Roman officer] whom history has not named. On his own initiative, he diverted 20 maniples from a point where victory was already assured, to surprise the enemy phalanx in the rear.[18]

Unable to wheel their huge pikes around quickly enough to protect their backs, the Greek troops were slaughtered in their ranks. The Roman legions were even more successful against the phalanx fielded at Pydna, in northern Greece, in the Third Macedonian War in 168.

The Battle of Pydna sounded the death knell of Greek resistance against Rome, for by this time the Greek Seleucid kingdom, centered in the Near East, had already fallen to Roman steel; and only a year later, the Ptolemaic kingdom, made up largely of Egypt, wisely submitted to Rome without a fight. The Egyptians then became Roman vassals, allowed to handle their own domestic affairs as long as they did Rome's bidding in the international scene. In the short space of a century, the seemingly unstoppable wave of Roman im-

The Macedonian phalanx in action. Developed by King Philip II in the fourth century B.C., this formation dominated classical warfare for more than a century.

perialism had made the conceited boast of *mare nostrum* a stark reality. "The entire Mediterranean Sea was a Roman lake," remarks historian Naphtali Lewis, "and those who lived on and around it looked to Rome as the arbiter [decider] of their fortunes."[19]

The Piper Pays Rome

Being on the receiving end of Rome's imperialism was an intimidating and humiliating experience, especially for nations that had once been proud and mighty in their own right. Not surprisingly, therefore, envy and hatred of the Romans was common in their conquered vassal states. Egypt is a particularly fitting example, since its leaders, its principal city of Alexandria, and especially its fear and dislike of Rome would end up figuring heavily in the political and military events attending the fall of the Republic.

Egypt had once been one of the world's most magnificent and powerful kingdoms. But in the centuries during which Rome was rising to prominence in Italy, Egyptian civilization had declined and fallen under the yoke of foreign conquerors. One of these conquerors was the Greek general Alexander the Great, who in the fourth century B.C. created the largest empire the world had yet seen. In 332, he marched into Egypt and soon afterward founded the city of Alexandria (naming it after himself), on the Nile delta. This stately port rapidly became the busiest and most prosperous in the ancient world. Only a few years after establishing the city, Alexander died unexpectedly; almost immediately his generals began fighting one another for control of his empire.[20] After a series of long, bloody, and costly wars, some of these men established the large Greek kingdoms that would later fall to Rome. In Egypt, Ptolemy founded the Greek Ptolemaic dynasty, the royal line that would eventually produce the legendary Cleopatra VII.

The Ptolemies ran Egypt just as it had traditionally been run, as an absolute monarchy. Apart from the fact that the ruling family was now Greek, essentially nothing in the life of an average Egyptian was different. Most people were impoverished and uneducated and toiled ceaselessly in the fields, on state building projects, or in state-owned mines. By contrast, the Ptolemaic monarchs, their families, and their small circle of noble attendants enjoyed happy lives of opulence and leisure. They ate the best foods, wore beautiful clothes, and, thanks to a small army of slaves and servants, never had to perform work or physical labor of any kind.

But the comfortable, apparently powerful position the Ptolemies enjoyed in time proved to be largely an illusion. Once Rome had made Egypt its vassal, Egyptian leaders had to face the fact that they ruled over a third-rate power with no real control over its own destiny. They realized that Rome could at any moment flex its military muscle and directly annex Egypt. Cowed and humiliated, one Ptolemy after another tried to prevent such an occurrence by, in effect, groveling before the Roman leadership.

One Ptolemy who groveled more than most of his predecessors was Cleopatra's father, King Ptolemy XII, popularly called Auletes, "the Piper," because of his skill as a flute player. Auletes ascended the Egyptian

Alexander the Great lies on his deathbed. Among his generals, later called the "Successors," was Ptolemy, who established the Greek Ptolemaic dynasty in Egypt.

throne in 80 B.C. He proved to be an inept administrator who tried to make up for his financial blunders by imposing massive new taxes on his people, a policy that eventually pushed them to the brink of open rebellion. Auletes hated the Romans. But he was not above making whatever deals were necessary to maintain his local authority. In 59, he attempted to strengthen that authority by getting the most powerful Romans of the day to recognize him publicly as the rightful ruler of Egypt. The title he sought was "Friend and Ally" of the Roman people, which, he hoped, would make him a more feared figure in his own land and thereby prevent imminent rebellion. Auletes received this much coveted title, but only after paying two Roman notables a huge bribe, which thrust him deeply into debt. And even then his throne was not secure. While he was visiting Rome in 57, his daughter, Cleopatra's sister, seized power. With Roman help, Auletes eventually managed to regain his throne, but soon afterward he died an unhappy and broken man.

An Invitation to Adventurers

Auletes was likely unaware that the Roman notables with whom he had sealed his bargain—Julius Caesar and Gnaeus Pompey—were among a new breed of Roman leaders whose actions were already eroding the foundations of the Republic. In centuries past, of course, the Senate had largely run the show in Rome. The consuls and other generals and public officials had given their allegiance to the state, as had the armies themselves. But near the beginning of the fateful first century B.C. this situation began to change. The army evolved from a militia-like force made up mostly of landowners into a more professional force composed of volunteers from all classes. These largely less affluent, less educated masses of soldiers, comments historian F. R. Cowell, were more

> excitable and unsteady, [and] ready to back almost any man who would offer them land and bread. They were

therefore a standing invitation to political adventurers. . . . Any man having military supremacy, that is to say, a sufficiently large force of Roman soldiers willing to follow him through thick and thin, could easily have political supremacy also if he wanted it.[21]

One such adventurer, the first of the series of military strongmen who would end up toppling the Republic, was the popular general Gaius Marius (Julius

Peacock and Honey Cakes Instead of Porridge

The Romans of the early Republic were generally conservative, austere, and averse to luxury and excess. But toward the end of the republican times, having gained a world empire and the great wealth that came with it, those who could afford it became more indulgent. In this excerpt from A Noise of War, *A. J. Langguth describes how the meals at parties given by and for the upper classes were often both appetizing and wasteful.*

"After centuries of austerity, wealthy Romans had discovered that a meal could be more appetizing than a simple bowl of wheat porridge. Dinner parties now started after an hour or two at a public bath and ended with extended rounds of drinking. Throughout the meal, guests lay on cushions, propped up on an elbow. Because the menu was certain to be rich, [some] Romans excused themselves during a banquet to vomit so they would be able to consume the courses to follow. Purging was considered a polite way to compliment a host. Appetizers of oysters, eggs, and sardines were washed down by wine sweetened with honey. Six or seven main dishes followed: mackerel, mullet, eels and prawns [shrimp], goose, ostrich, chicken and—if the host could afford it—peacock. The meats might be lamb, suckling pig, hare and wild goat. Desserts included a variety of fruit and honeyed cakes. Ranks of servants stood by to keep the wine glasses filled. To those excesses, Sulla [an aristocrat who used force to make himself dictator in the 80s B.C.] brought his own insatiable appetite. For his banquets, he ordered far more food than his guests could consume, until haunches of uneaten meat were dumped every day into the Tiber along with his enemies' corpses."

Caesar's uncle), who served the first of his many consulships in 107 B.C. Of Marius's important military reforms and the unprecedented degree of loyalty his troops felt for him, scholar A. J. Langguth writes:

> Marius's true strength was not simply his popularity with the civilians [who had elected him consul], it was the loyalty of his troops. Over his career, Marius had set about making Rome's army more professional. . . . [He] eliminated the last property requirements for service and made every citizen eligible. To replace the unpopular practice of drafting farmers, he began calling for volunteers among the city's poor and quickly drew as many troops as he needed. Men now signed up for a specific term, not simply until a campaign ended. Under Marius, volunteers took their oath of allegiance to the general, not to that year's consuls. . . . Soldiering was a rough, disciplined life, and the men who chose it became Rome's sinew. Peasants from Italy or Crete [the large island lying southeast of Greece] or the Balearic Islands [in the western Mediterranean], they were men with no standing in Rome who had discovered a powerful trade to ply. Their loyalty to

After military strongman Gaius Marius reformed the Roman military, soldiers swore allegiance to their generals rather than to the state.

a commander outweighed anything they felt for an abstraction like the Roman Republic.[22]

Setting a precedent that other strongmen would follow, Marius used his power, wealth, and political connections to secure handsome pensions of land and money for his retiring troops. In doing so, the generals exploited the fact that the Roman government had not seen fit to provide such pensions on a regular basis, despite the necessity of maintaining a strong, loyal army to protect Rome's vast realm. In this respect, Roman politicians had failed and they would pay a terrible price for that failure. With their own personal armies at their disposal, men like Marius could, in theory, challenge the government and even march on the capital itself. Unfortunately for the Republic and its proud traditions, theory would become reality in Marius's own lifetime; Rome's voracious appetite for war, previously satisfied by pursuing a policy of foreign imperialism, would soon turn inward and begin devouring its own vital organs.

Chapter

2 Strongmen and Civil Strife: The Struggle to Maintain Order

The first century B.C. had barely opened when ominous cracks began appearing in the Republic's structure. Some of the gathering troubles were political in nature. In their recent conquests the Romans had amassed tremendous political and military power and influence throughout most of the known world, as well as great wealth. But they now began to see that administering such large and far-flung territories was no easy task. Their constitution (a collection of laws and political conventions rather than a written document) and government had originally been designed to rule a single city-state inhabited by one people. This system did not work nearly as well on the scale of a vast collection of nations composed of many diverse peoples. As a result, Rome encountered an increasingly difficult struggle to maintain order in its empire.

The struggle was increasingly internal as well as external as military strongmen vied for control of the state itself. Though Marius had effected the political and military reforms that had led to the rise of the generals, he himself never attempted to usurp governmental power. That ugly precedent was set by one of Marius's assistants, L. Cornelius Sulla. Several other ambitious individuals, including Marius's illustrious nephew Caesar, soon followed

Sulla's example, plunging the government, nation, and empire into one crisis after another.

Making Italy a True Nation

That Rome's republican system was increasingly inadequate to the task of governing large populations of conquered peoples was demonstrated in the first century B.C.'s first round of civil strife, the Social War.[23] The inability, or in some cases refusal, of the upper-class men who ran the Republic to deal with growing unrest among Rome's Italian allies showed how the once-flexible and amenable government had become inflexible and insensitive to people's needs. As James Breasted explains, the allies

> had contributed as many troops to the conquering armies as had Rome herself, and now they were refused any voice in the control of the conquered territory or any share in the immense wealth which they saw the Romans drawing from it. The wise and liberal policy of the ancient Senate in freely granting citizenship to communities in newly acquired Italian territory had

been long abandoned. . . . Before the different communities of Italy had had time to merge into a nation, they had been forced into a long series of foreign wars which had made vast conquests. But possession of these conquests had blinded the Senate and the governing community at Rome. By this sudden wealth and power Rome had been raised above all feeling of fellowship with other communities of Italy. The great peninsula was filled with disunited communities, and there now rested on Rome the obligation to make Italy a [true] nation.[24]

The Social War began in 90 B.C. when a Roman praetor, or judge, his assistant, and several other Roman citizens were murdered by rebels in the town of Asculum, in the eastern Apennine foothills of south-central Italy. Emboldened by the news, many other towns in the southern

A likeness of Cornelius Sulla, who declared himself dictator of Rome after defeating Marius's forces in a brief but bloody civil war.

half of the peninsula rebelled; some of them formed a collective government and even established a new capital, which they called Italica. The surprised and outraged Senate sent several Roman commanders against the rebels in the following year, overall to little effect. By early 88, after thousands on both sides had died in bitter fighting, the senators conceded the practical necessity of granting the former allies citizenship. A sweeping decree declared that all free adult males in Italy south of the Po Valley were hereby full Roman citizens. This move had the desired effect of inducing most of the rebels to lay down their arms; a few held out against government forces for a few months, but by early 87 all of these, including Asculum, had been recaptured.

Rome had managed to survive the Social War only by giving in to the rebels' principal demand—the granting of citizenship rights. The effects of the conflict were both good and bad. On the positive side, the future threat of revolt by Italian peoples had been virtually eliminated; Italy was at last a single, strong nation united under Rome; and the recruiting ground for native Roman legions was now much larger, which meant that the government could raise larger armies. On the negative side, the recruiting possibilities for military adventurers were also larger. In addition, military historian Lawrence Keppie points out,

> [an] immediate, though less obvious consequence was that the Social War left many men embittered and homeless. Often these found a new home in the legions, adding to the increasing element of "professionals," and infusing a spirit of callousness and indifference,

which was to have serious consequences later. It may be that the Social War did more to engender the grasping, greedy soldiery of the Late Republic than any of Marius's reforms.[25]

Marius Versus Sulla

If the Roman governing elite believed the citizenship decree had created lasting order in the country, they were sadly mistaken. A second and even worse round of civil strife followed hot on the heels of the first. Marius's powerful and aristocratic assistant, Sulla, was elected consul in the year following the decree and the Senate assigned him an army to quell a threat to Roman interests in Asia Minor. But the leaders of the popular party, who dominated the Assembly and who had become openly hostile to the aristocratic senators, cried foul. They wanted their own favorite, Marius, who had been born a commoner and risen by merit through the ranks, to lead the eastern campaign.

As tensions between the popular and aristocratic factions swiftly rose, Sulla struck first; he marched an army into the capital, marking the first time that a Roman consul had seized control of Rome by force. He then pushed through a law that forbade the Assembly from voting on any measure without the Senate's consent. Having hamstrung the popular party and greatly strengthened the Senate and aristocracy, he departed with his troops for Asia Minor.

Roman fights Roman in a massive bloodbath as Sulla and his veterans smash their way into the Roman capital.

With Sulla gone, his opponents grew bolder and sporadic fighting erupted in the streets of the capital. In the hours that followed, the Senate's local garrison of troops overreacted and began killing citizens in the Forum, the city's main square; but suddenly Marius appeared at the head of his loyal cavalry and began a counterattack that turned into a massacre of many in the aristocratic faction. Now an old man, Marius died soon afterward. But his supporters remained in power, waiting anxiously for the day of reckoning when Sulla would return from the east.

That day came in 83 B.C. Sulla marched on Rome a second time and won a bloody contest against his enemies at the very gates of the city. Once in control of the capital, he took the unprecedented action of making himself dictator, and not long afterward he began a series of bloody purges of Marius's supporters and their families. According to the first-century A.D. Greek historian and biographer Plutarch:

> Sulla now devoted himself entirely to the work of butchery. The city was filled with murder and there was no counting the executions or setting a limit to them. Many people were killed because of purely personal ill feeling; they had no connection with Sulla in any way, but Sulla, in order to gratify members of his own party, permitted them to be done away with. . . . Without consulting any magistrate, Sulla published a list of eighty men to be condemned. Public opinion was horrified, but, after a single day's interval, he published another list containing 220 more names, and next day a third list with the same number of names on

it. And in a public speech . . . he said that he was publishing the names of all those whom he happened to remember: those who escaped his memory for the moment would have their names put up later. He also condemned anyone who sheltered or attempted to save a person whose name was on the lists. Death was the penalty for such acts of humanity, and there were no exceptions in the cases of brothers, sons, or parents.[26]

Sulla also murdered a number of well-to-do people, including, to the surprise of many, aristocrats; he then confiscated their money and distributed it to his troops to keep their loyalty. Plutarch writes:

> Those who were killed in the passion of the moment or because of some private hatred were as nothing compared with those who were butchered for the sake of their property. In fact it became a regular thing to say among the executioners that "So-and-so was killed by his big mansion, so-and-so by his gardens, so-and-so by his hot-water installation [private baths]."[27]

The New Group of Strongmen

Luckily for Rome, Sulla's reign of terror was brief. He retired and died in 78 and within a few years the government and the capital had returned to business as usual; that is, with one important exception. Sulla's civil war and dictatorship demonstrated that the government was unable to maintain order, whereas the army, under a charismatic individual, clearly was. An ominous precedent had been set, pointing the way for other ambitious, powerful men to manipulate the apparatus of state.

The new group of political-military strongmen who rose to prominence in the three decades following Sulla's death were also motivated by the desire to further their personal careers and prestige. The most powerful and famous of these, Gnaeus Pompey, Marcus Crassus, and Julius Caesar, disliked and distrusted one another, and each was perfectly willing to destroy the others to achieve his goals. But they also did not hesitate to work together when it became feasible for their combined resources to bring the government to its knees.

During the tumultuous years of their power struggles with the Republic, and with one another, only one influential man—Cicero—had the courage and integrity to oppose them openly and to fight to maintain the traditional government. Although he blamed them for the chaos and bloodshed their selfish and ruthless quest for power caused, he also blamed himself and his senatorial colleagues for failing to stop the rise of the generals in the first place. In 49 B.C., with a devastating civil war raging around him, he wrote to his friend Atticus:

> Do you see the kind of man into whose hands the state has fallen? . . . The people of the country towns and the farmers talk to me a great deal. They care for nothing at all but their lands, their little homesteads, and their tiny fortunes. And see how public opinion has changed: they fear the man they once trusted and adore the man they

Marcus Tullius Cicero—lawyer, orator, statesman, and the last great champion of Rome's republican government.

once dreaded. It pains me to think of the mistakes and wrongs of ours that are responsible for this reaction.[28]

Until the bitter end, Cicero believed in the possibility of turning back the clock and putting the generals in their place;

sadly, however, without the backing of the armies, his valiant struggle was doomed from the start.

The Rise of Pompey and Crassus

Of the powerful generals and politicians whose policies Cicero opposed, Pompey was the first to attempt to fill the power vacuum left when Sulla died. One of Sulla's most trusted subordinates, Pompey won a number of battles against Marius's supporters during the Sullan-Marian civil war. Only in his midtwenties at the time, Pompey quickly earned a reputation as a daring and able soldier and became popular with many senators and other aristocrats. In 77 B.C. the Senate assigned him the important task of leading an army to Spain to put down a rebellion instigated by one of Marius's former supporters. In the months and years that followed, news of Pompey's successful campaigns impressed and excited Romans of all walks of life.

While Pompey was away in Spain, Crassus searched for his own opportunity to win fame, glory, and power. Already the wealthiest man in Rome, his fortune earned through silver mines and real estate ventures, Crassus hoped for a crisis that would allow him to take command of an army. Just such a situation arose in 73, when a group of slaves at a gladiator school in Capua, about a hundred miles south of Rome, escaped and began terrorizing the surrounding countryside. They were led by a slave named Spartacus. According to Plutarch, the slaves

had done nothing wrong, but, simply because of the cruelty of their owner, were kept in close confinement until the time came for them to engage in combat. Two hundred of them planned to escape, but their plan was betrayed and only seventy-eight . . . managed to act in time and get away, armed with choppers and spits which they seized from some cookhouse. On the road they came across some wagons which were carrying arms for gladiators to another city, and they took these arms for their own use. They then occupied a strong position and elected three leaders. The first [chief] of these was Spartacus. . . . [He] not only had a great spirit and great physical strength, but was, much

An idealized portrait of Pompey (106–48 B.C.). According to Plutarch, Pompey had "a venerable and princely air."

more than one would expect from his condition [i.e., slavery], most intelligent and cultured.[29]

Spartacus freed many slaves in central Italy, built a formidable army from their ranks, and defeated several small Roman armies sent against him. The government became increasingly fearful that he might free every slave in Italy and march on Rome itself. Realizing that the most popular general of the day, Pompey, was away in Spain, Crassus seized the moment and volunteered to put down the rebellious slaves.

But Crassus soon found that he had undertaken a task more challenging than he had expected. Tens of thousands of slaves had eagerly turned on their masters and joined the slave army. Moreover, Spartacus and his fellows from the Capua school were teaching many of the slaves to fight like gladiators, making them more than a match for Roman troops. By the time Crassus took the field with his army in 72, the slaves numbered over ninety thousand, many of them well armed. As might be expected under these circumstances, at first Crassus did not fare well against the slaves. One of his officers was badly defeated in a skirmish; and then Crassus received the added unwelcome news that Pompey, having achieved complete victory in Spain, was on his way back to Rome. To ensure that he himself would get all the credit for defeating Spartacus, Crassus desperately tried to provoke a major battle with the slaves before Pompey arrived.

Crassus caught up with the slave army in 71 in the southern Italian region of Lucania. There, Spartacus and his followers staged a heroic last stand; but they ultimately went down to defeat and Spartacus himself died fighting.[30] Crassus fought well himself. But unfortunately for him, Pompey and his own army arrived just in time to take most of the credit for the victory. As Plutarch puts it:

> Crassus had had good fortune, had shown excellent generalship, and had risked his own life in the fighting; nevertheless the success of Crassus served to increase the fame of Pompey. The fugitives from the battle fell in with Pompey's troops and were destroyed, so that Pompey, in his dispatch to the Senate, was able to say that, while Crassus had certainly conquered the slaves in open battle, he himself had dug the war up by the roots.[31]

As for the six thousand surviving slaves, the victors crucified them along the road to Rome as a warning to others contemplating rebellion.

Caesar Enters the Game

In the early 60s B.C., Pompey and Crassus remained the most prominent figures in Rome. In particular, Pompey's reputation soared higher than ever after he cleared the entire Mediterranean of pirates in a brilliant, lightning campaign in 67. Yet he and Crassus did not go completely unchallenged in these and the years that followed, for Cicero gained increasing popularity as a champion both of the people and of the republican government. In the consular election of 63, Cicero dared to oppose the candidates supported by Crassus, and to the surprise of many aristocrats, Cicero won.

Pompey and the Pirates

In this excerpt from the Life of Pompey *(from his* Lives*), Plutarch describes one of the famous general's most legendary exploits— the swift destruction of the Mediterranean pirate menace, an operation in which he burned some thirteen hundred pirate vessels and captured four hundred more, all without the loss of a single Roman ship.*

"The power of the pirates extended over the whole area of our Mediterranean sea. The result was that all navigation and all commerce were at a standstill; and it was this aspect of the situation which caused the Romans . . . to send out Pompey with a commission to drive the pirates off the seas. . . . Pompey was to be given not only the supreme naval command but what amounted in fact to an absolute authority and uncontrolled power over everyone. The law provided that his command should extend over the sea as far as the pillars of Hercules [Strait of Gibraltar] and over all the mainland to the distance of fifty miles from the sea. . . . Then he was . . . given power to . . . take from the treasury and from the taxation officials as much money as he wanted, to raise a fleet of 200 ships, and to arrange personally for the levying of troops and sailors in whatever numbers he thought fit. . . . He divided the Mediterranean and the adjacent coasts into thirteen separate areas, each of which he entrusted to a commander with a fixed number of ships. This disposal of his forces throughout the sea enabled him to surround entire fleets of pirate ships, which he hunted down and brought into harbor. . . . All this was done in the space of forty days."

Almost immediately after his election victory, Cicero met and overcame his greatest challenge—the saving of the Republic from another military takeover. Hearing that Lucius Sergius Catilina, popularly known as Catiline, a patrician and former colleague of Crassus's, was plotting to kill the consuls and seize the government, Cicero acted swiftly and boldly. In a series of powerful speeches, Cicero convinced the Senate to grant him and his fellow consul, Antonius, all powers necessary to foil the plot. Early in 62, Antonius attacked and defeated the small army Catiline was raising for his coup, killing the would-be usurper; meanwhile, Cicero arrested Catiline's accomplices in Rome and ordered their immediate execution.

The rescue of the government made Cicero the man of the hour. But the reality was that he had defeated only a bungling, third-rate strongman. The two first-rate strongmen, Pompey and Crassus,

Cicero, his hands upraised for dramatic emphasis, stands before his fellow senators and denounces Catiline, who sits alone, shunned by the others, at lower right.

were still as powerful as ever; and the man who would turn out to be stronger than all of them was even now entering the Roman power game. In the same year that Cicero won the consulship, Julius Caesar was elected praetor. In this and other public offices gained in preceding years, Caesar had already begun to display the remarkable tactical skills that would characterize his later political and military maneuvers. He showed that he was capable of courting the popular support of the masses and at the same time of making the backroom deals necessary to win over the rich and powerful. In the latter case, this meant dealing with Pompey and Crassus. Caesar was well aware that the influ-

ence these towering figures wielded constituted a significant obstacle in the path of any ambitious politician. Working with rather than against these men, he decided, would help to clear his way to the summit of state power.

To that end, sometime in the summer of 60 B.C., probably shortly before the consular elections (for the following year of 59), Caesar engineered a secret alliance with Pompey and then approached Crassus. Crassus made no bones about his dislike for Pompey and also undoubtedly envied and feared Caesar's obvious abilities and ambitions. But like the other two men, Crassus saw the wisdom of the alliance. Singly, each of them lacked the resources to override the Senate; but by combining their wealth and influence they could conceivably manipulate the government to their own ends. And so was born the uneasy but tremendously powerful partnership that later came to be known as the First Triumvirate.

The triumvirate proved its power almost immediately, for with Pompey's and Crassus's backing, Caesar ran for and easily won the consulship. His entire term as consul in the year 59 was marked by bullying, intimidation, and illegal tactics. He regularly cut shady deals, ignored or violated laws and legislative procedure, and through the threat of force silenced nearly all opposition. All the while, he and his fellow triumvirs grew richer, and, like ruthless gangsters, used bribes and fear to spread their power and influence throughout the government and other social institutions. Cicero and other staunch republicans had long worried that the rise of powerful individuals might threaten or even destroy the state. The advent of the triumvirate transformed that worry into alarm. Summing up this new political reality, historian Ernle Bradford remarks, "From the moment that these three men had decided to pool their resources—

Cicero Exposes Catiline

Here is the dramatic opening of the first of Cicero's speeches against Catiline (quoted in Selected Political Speeches of Cicero)*, in which the great orator exposed the plot against the government. Cicero delivered the speech with Catiline himself sitting before him in the Senate chamber.*

"In the name of heaven, Catilina, how long will you exploit our patience? Surely your insane activities cannot escape our retaliation forever! Are there to be no limits to this swaggering, ungovernable recklessness? The garrison which guards the Palatine [hill] by night, the patrols ranging the city, the terror that grips the population, the amassing of all loyal citizens on one single spot, this meeting of the Senate behind strongly fortified defenses, the expressions on the countenances of each man here—have none of these sights made the slightest impact on your heart? You must be well aware that your plot has been detected. Now that every single person in this place knows all about your conspiracy, you cannot fail to realize it is doomed. . . . What a scandalous commentary on our age and its standards! For the Senate knows all about these things. The consul sees them being done. And yet this man [Catiline] still lives! Lives? He walks right into the Senate. He joins in our national debates—watches and notes and marks down with his gaze each one of us he plots to assassinate."

military power and fame, monetary power, and political genius—the end of the Republic was in sight."[32]

"The Die Is Cast"

Trying to avert what he saw as a potential disaster in the making, Cicero bravely spoke out against the triumvirs. He argued that the Roman government had not been founded by and for a few individuals, but was the result of generations of Romans working together for the common good. He called upon Roman leaders, including Caesar and his colleagues, to recognize their duty to the state. But these words of moderation fell on deaf ears. The triumvirs continued to intimidate the government; moreover, to rid themselves of Cicero they accused him of abusing his former consular powers. To avoid prosecution and what would have been, under the prevailing political climate, certain conviction, Cicero went into hiding in Greece.

The great republican champion had been right about a disaster in the making, for in the years to come Rome would suffer far worse abuses than those perpetrated by the triumvirate. When his term as consul ended, Caesar used his influence to get himself appointed proconsul, or governor, of the province of Transalpine Gaul, now southern France. He realized that he still lacked military experience and backing to match Pompey's and reasoned that he could acquire both while conquering the still wild non-Roman lands of central and northern Gaul. During eight years of hard and often brilliant campaigning, Caesar achieved his goal,

building a loyal personal army of thirteen legions, a total of more than fifty thousand battle-hardened troops. His Gallic conquests also added huge territories to the empire, further bolstering his popularity and political power.

While in Gaul, Caesar had kept himself informed of events in Rome. By 50 B.C., the government and parts of the city were in a state of near chaos. Three years before, Crassus had sought glory and bolstered status by leading a military campaign in the east, but he had died in battle, leaving Pompey the only triumvir left in the capital. Though a skilled general, Pompey was a poor administrator, and he in effect stood by and did nothing as rival factions in the government stirred up mobs and riots. He also allowed himself to become the tool of conservative senators who sought to destroy the remainder of the triumvirate by pitting him and Caesar against each other. In January 49, the Senate declared Pompey the state's protector and Caesar a public enemy. Caesar was ordered to disband his army at once; when his assistant in Rome, Mark Antony, protested, some senators threatened his life and forced him from the city.

Learning of these events, Caesar boldly asserted himself. In defiance of the Senate, on January 7, 49, he led his troops to the Rubicon River, the formal boundary between the Gallic provinces and Italy proper. According to the later Roman historian Suetonius, Caesar told his officers, "We may still draw back but, once across that little bridge, we shall have to fight it out. . . . Let us accept [the signs] from the gods, and follow where they beckon, in vengeance on our doubling-dealing enemies. The die is cast."[33] With these

Caesar leads his men across the Rubicon River, the traditional border between Cisalpine Gaul and Italy proper. This fateful act ignited a destructive civil war that dragged on for five years.

words, Caesar crossed the Rubicon and plunged the Roman world into a new and disastrous civil war.

Caesar Becomes Dictator

The new conflict and the events that followed it proved momentous for Rome. As Caesar marched on the capital at the head of his huge army, Pompey, the consuls, and many senators fled. Pompey went to Greece to raise an army to oppose his former colleague and the following year, on the plain of Pharsalus, in east-central Greece, the two greatest living generals clashed. Caesar won the day, despite the fact that his army was only half as large as his opponent's, forcing Pompey to flee once again, this time to Egypt. There, Pompey met a treacherous death at the hands of the young king, Ptolemy XIII (Auletes' son), and his royal advisers. They hoped to gain Caesar's favor by this deed; but their plan backfired as Caesar sided with Ptolemy's ambitious and politically shrewd sister, Cleopatra, in a short but bloody dynastic civil war. Ptolemy paid dearly for challenging Roman might, ending up as a corpse floating in the Nile.

Leaving his new ally (and lover) firmly in power in Egypt, Caesar returned to Rome. Militarily and politically, his position was firm and unchallenged, and he might have used his tremendous powers to lead the Roman commonwealth into a new and constructive era. Instead, he outraged many old-guard republicans by declaring himself dictator for life,

Caesar's "Strange Delusion"

In this tract from On Duties *(quoted in Lewis and Reinhold's* Roman Civilization) *composed after Caesar's assassination, Cicero is bluntly critical of the dead leader's seemingly kingly goals.*

"Our tyrant deserved his death for having made an exception of the one thing that was the blackest crime of all. Why do we gather instances of petty crime [committed by Caesar]—legacies criminally obtained and fraudulent buying and selling? Behold, here you have a man who was ambitious to be king of the Roman people and master of the whole world; and he achieved it! The man who maintains that such a position is morally right is a madman, for he justifies the destruction of law and liberty and thinks their hideous and detestable suppression glorious. But if anyone agrees that it is not morally right to be king in a state that once was free and that ought to be free now . . . with what remonstrance [pleadings] or rather with what appeal should I try to tear him away from so strange a delusion? For, O ye immortal gods! can the most horrible and hideous of all murders—that of fatherland—bring advantage to anybody, even though he who has committed such a crime receives from his enslaved fellow citizens the title of 'Father of his Country'?"

Julius Caesar's head is graced by a laurel wreath, an ancient symbol of victory, honor, and glory.

transacting business on a throne of ivory and gold, and accepting religious dedications that referred to him as a god. Fearing that he would go a step further and declare himself king, a title most Romans heartily despised, a group of senators led by Gaius Cassius and Marcus Brutus took

desperate action. Their now famous attack occurred in the Senate chamber on March 15, 44 B.C. According to Suetonius:

As soon as Caesar took his seat the conspirators crowded around him as if to pay their respects. Tillius Cimber

. . . came up close, pretending to ask a question. Caesar made a gesture of postponement, but Cimber caught hold of his shoulders. "This is violence!" Caesar cried, and . . . as he turned away, one of the Casca brothers with a sweep of his dagger stabbed him just below the throat. . . . Twenty-three dagger thrusts went home as he stood there. Caesar did not utter a sound after Casca's blow had drawn a groan from him; though some say that when he saw Marcus Brutus about to deliver the second blow, he reproached him in Greek with: "You, too, my child?" The entire Senate then dispersed in confusion, and Caesar was left lying dead for some time until three slave boys carried him home in a litter, with one arm hanging over the side.[34]

After the assassination, the conspirators ran into the streets proclaiming liberty; they thought that by killing Caesar they had restored the integrity and power of their beloved Republic. But they naïvely failed to recognize that it was the government's very lack of authority and flexibility that had allowed Caesar and other ambitious men to intimidate it. His demise only created a sudden but temporary vacuum at the elite pinnacle of Roman power politics. A new generation of power-hungry and self-serving individuals would soon move to fill that vacuum; and in so doing they would plunge the already mortally wounded Republic into its final death agonies.

Chapter

3 A "Superb and Terrible" Struggle: The Rise of Antony and Octavian

The two years following Caesar's assassination were uncertain and turbulent ones for Rome, and indeed for the whole Mediterranean world. Several factions and individuals emerged and vied to fill the power vacuum created by Caesar's demise. On the one hand were the conspirators who had killed the dictator. This group, led by Brutus and Cassius, wanted to restore the authority of the Senate and the honor of the Republic and to keep the government safe from power-hungry men like Caesar. Cicero, of course, was also a strong advocate of the republican system; but he had wisely kept a cool head and refrained from joining the assassination plot. He knew full well that the ambitious men his colleagues feared already had and would continue to wield enough military might to overshadow the Senate. His strategy, therefore, was to strike deals with various powerful parties and factions in the hope that his actions would strengthen, or at least preserve, the traditional government.

The first of these powerful parties stepped forward immediately after Caesar's death. He was Caesar's former assistant, Mark Antony, a capable general but a mediocre and untrustworthy administrator with a reputation for heavy drinking and womanizing. According to Plutarch:

In his youth, it is said, Antony gave promise of a brilliant future, but then he became a close friend of Curio [another of Caesar's assistants] and this association seems to have fallen like a blight upon his career. Curio was a man who had become wholly enslaved to the demands of pleasure, and in order to make Antony more pliable to his will, he plunged him into a life of drinking bouts, love-affairs, and reckless spending.[35]

Following Antony in succeeding weeks, Caesar's adopted son (and great-nephew), Octavian, and a popular general named Marcus Lepidus also stepped forward to claim pieces of the state pie. Meanwhile, in Egypt, Cleopatra watched in calculated silence as events unfolded in distant Rome. She shrewdly planned to hold back, let the Roman men fight it out, and then somehow attach herself and her own country's fortunes to the victor.

The months following Caesar's murder would witness all of these factions jockeying for position. New armies would be raised and the Roman world would once again become polarized into opposing camps in preparation for civil war. During this anxious and suspenseful period, no one could say for sure who the ultimate winner would be. What was clear to almost everyone, however, was that when the dust finally settled, Rome's old republican government would be significantly and permanently altered.

Antony's Scheme Pays Off

In fact, mere hours after striking Caesar down, the conspirators' dream of restoring senatorial power collapsed like a house of cards around them. To the anxious citizens who had gathered near the Senate after the murder, Brutus and Cassius had given assurances that they had killed Caesar for the good of Rome, to prevent the dictator from denying the people their constitutional freedoms.

"When a large crowd had assembled," writes Plutarch in his *Life of Brutus,*

> Brutus made a speech which was calculated to suit the occasion and please the people. His audience applauded him loudly and called upon him to come down from the Capitol, and the conspirators, their confidence returning, now made their way to the Forum. . . . [There] the crowd which faced him [Brutus] was an audience of mixed sympathies and had come prepared to raise a riot, but at the sight of Brutus it was overcome with awe and awaited his words in orderly silence.[36]

But the assassins had not bargained on Antony's powers to sway the local populace to his own purposes. At first, to put the conspirators off their guard, he

Slaves carry Caesar's body across the Roman Forum. According to ancient historians, Caesar sustained twenty-three knife wounds.

pretended to support them, going so far as to invite Cassius over for dinner and to persuade the Senate to consider granting the conspirators amnesty. Then, as Plutarch tells it, when they least expected it he struck them a mortal blow.

It so happened that when Caesar's body was carried out for burial, Antony delivered the customary eulogy over it in the Forum. When he saw that his oratory had cast a spell over the people and that they were deeply stirred by his words, he began to introduce into his praises a note of pity and of indignation at Caesar's fate. Finally, at the close of his speech, he snatched up the dead man's robe and brandished it aloft, all blood-stained as it was and stabbed through in many places, and called those who had done the deed murderers and villains. This appeal had such an effect on the people that they piled up benches and tables and burned Caesar's body in the Forum, and then, snatching up firebrands from the pyre, they ran to the houses of his assassins and attacked them.[37]

Antony's scheme paid off. Hearing of the approach of the angry crowds, the conspirators fled the city; most escaped Italy entirely and took refuge in Greece,

This 1881 woodcut captures the dramatic moment in Act III, scene 2 of Shakespeare's play Julius Caesar, in which Mark Antony reveals Caesar's blood-soaked body, shocking and saddening the crowd gathered to hear the eulogy.

"I Loved Rome More"

Because it was based on works by Plutarch and other ancient writers, William Shakespeare's 1599 play Julius Caesar *dramatized mainly real characters and events, including Antony's funeral oration over Caesar's body. Less famous, but equally eloquent, is this speech, preceding Antony's, in which Brutus justifies Caesar's assassination to the Roman mob.*

"BRUTUS. Romans, countrymen, and lovers, hear me for my cause, and be silent, that you may hear. Believe me for mine honor, and have respect to mine honor, that you may believe. Censure me in your wisdom, and awake your senses, that you may the better judge. If there be any in this assembly, any dear friend of Caesar's, to him I say that Brutus's love to Caesar was no less than his. If then that friend demand why Brutus rose against Caesar, this is my answer: Not that I loved Caesar less, but that I loved Rome more. Had you rather that Caesar were living, and die all slaves, than that Caesar were dead, to live all free men? As Caesar loved me, I weep for him; as he was fortunate, I rejoice at it; as he was valiant, I honor him, but—as he was ambitious, I slew him. There is tears for his love; joy for his fortune; honor for his valor; and death for his ambition. Who is here so base that would be a bondman? If any, speak, for him have I offended. Who is here so rude that would not be a Roman? If any, speak, for him have I offended. Who is here so vile that will not love his country? If any, speak, for him have I offended. I pause for reply.

ALL. None, Brutus, none!

BRUTUS. Then none have I offended."

where Brutus and Cassius began raising troops with which they hoped to defeat Antony and restore their own prestige and authority.

This left Antony, at least for the moment, the most powerful figure in Rome. Cicero, who before Antony's swaying of the mob had advocated amnesty for the conspirators, now found himself in a dangerous position. Antony was a military ruffian who distrusted the Senate and particularly disliked Cicero, its most intellectual and respected member. If Cicero now asserted senatorial authority too vigorously, Antony might send his soldiers on a killing spree that would wipe out the remaining republican leadership. For the time being, therefore, Cicero and his colleagues laid low, waiting for someone else to risk openly challenging Antony.

"The Boy"

They did not have to wait long. In May 44 B.C. the news spread through Rome that Octavian had arrived to claim whatever inheritance his father, Caesar, had left him. Of course, no one at the time dreamed that Octavian, a sickly youth of nineteen with virtually no military experience, would present any credible threat to the formidable Antony. But "the boy," as Antony and others at the time mockingly referred to him, made up for his shortcomings with a shrewd and calculating mind. He immediately launched himself squarely into the world power game by publicly declaring that he was the "younger Caesar." According to classical scholar Henry T. Rowell, Octavian

> had proclaimed himself Caesar's son and heir and in one bold stroke had created for himself a reservoir of power. He had made himself the person around whom all those who were loyal to Caesar's memory and incensed by his unworthy end could rally. Caesar's veterans [in the army] had now found a new Caesar to whom they could transfer their devotion. . . . Caesar had died brutally murdered. . . . He now had a son to avenge the deed, and the magic name of Caesar was still alive.[38]

Apparently, Antony and the others contending for power did not at first grasp the significance of this act by Octavian. When the young man approached Antony and asked for his rightful inheritance—two-thirds of Caesar's estate—Antony thought he could be put off. Plutarch states:

Antony was at first inclined to despise Octavian as a mere boy, and told him that he must be out of his mind, adding the warning that a young man who possessed few influential friends and little experience of the world would find it a crushing burden to accept the inheritance and act as Caesar's executor. Octavian was quite unmoved by this argument and continued to demand the money, while Antony for his part did everything possible to humiliate him.[39]

Antony clearly had no inkling of the caliber of opponent he was up against. After being so rudely rebuffed, Octavian wasted no time in holding private meetings with and gaining the support of Cicero and other powerful leaders who despised Antony.

A bust of Mark Antony. He failed to realize the threat posed by young Octavian, who later proved to be a shrewd, determined, and dangerous opponent.

The young man's most necessary and important step, however, was to use the magic name of Caesar to back himself up with some real military muscle. Later, in his own synopsis of his deeds, the *Res gestae*, Octavian would declare matter-of-factly, "At the age of nineteen, I raised an army on my private initiative, and at my private expense, by means of which I liberated the state from the oppression of a tyrannical faction."[40] The "faction" to which he referred was, of course, Antony. In October 44, Octavian quickly gathered over three thousand of Caesar's veterans, and it became clear that he could easily hire many more if he so desired. In a deal with Cicero, he offered his and his army's services for the defense of the Senate against Antony. Finally realizing that Octavian represented a serious threat, Antony, unprepared for a major armed confrontation, fled to northern Italy.

The Second Triumvirate

With Antony out of the way, Octavian now demanded that the senators make the "younger Caesar" consul, the most powerful official post in the land. But Cicero and his colleagues refused. They had only been using Octavian to rid themselves of Antony and had no intention of allowing the young man to hold such a powerful post. But like Antony, they had severely underestimated Octavian's boldness and gutsy resolve. Without warning, he followed the lead of Sulla and Caesar by marching his new army into Rome; once more he made his demand—to be made consul—and this time the senators had no choice but to comply.

Octavian's next move showed again that he was politically wise beyond his years. In the past, many other leaders who had taken control of the capital, including Antony, had attempted to go it alone against other competing factions. Octavian realized that Antony, who was at that very moment raising troops of his own in the north, still posed a potent threat. Other military factions, the most significant led by Lepidus, might make their own bids for power at any time. The breakdown of the once solidly loyal Roman army into such undisciplined splinter factions was now quite common. "Its cause," the second-century A.D. Greek historian Appian correctly maintains,

> was that the generals, for the most part, as is usually the case in civil wars, were not regularly chosen [by the state]; that their armies were not drawn from the enrollment according to custom . . . that they did not serve the public so much as they did the individuals who brought them together; and that they served these [generals] not by the force of law, but by reason of private promises; not against the common enemy but against private foes—not against foreigners, but against fellow-citizens. . . . All these things impaired military discipline, and the soldiers thought that they were not so much serving in the army as lending assistance . . . to leaders who needed them for their own personal ends. . . . Understanding these facts, the generals tolerated such [lack of discipline], for they knew that their authority over their armies depended on bonuses rather than law.[41]

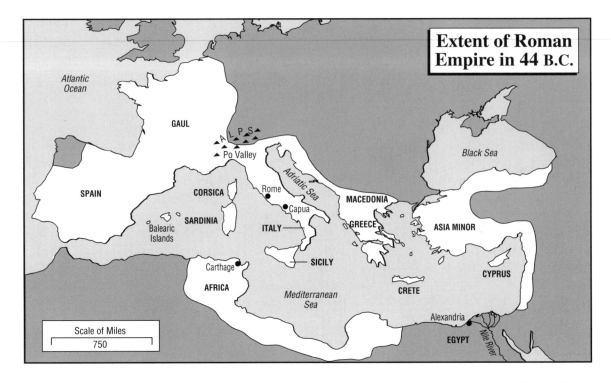

Extent of Roman Empire in 44 B.C.

Atlantic Ocean

GAUL

ALPS

Po Valley

SPAIN

CORSICA

Rome

Adriatic Sea

Black Sea

Capua

MACEDONIA

Balearic Islands

SARDINIA

ITALY

GREECE

ASIA MINOR

Carthage

SICILY

CYPRUS

AFRICA

Mediterranean Sea

CRETE

Alexandria

Nile River

EGYPT

Scale of Miles

750

In addition to the threat posed by such rival army factions, many of the Roman senators still secretly backed Brutus's and Cassius's republican forces, which were steadily gaining strength in Greece.

Taking on so many strong and diverse factions, Octavian reasoned, was foolhardy. So he took a lesson from his dead uncle. In creating the First Triumvirate, Caesar had allied himself with his main political opponents because no single faction, including the government, could stand up to their combined powers. In similar fashion, in the winter of 43 B.C. Octavian approached his own two strongest rivals, Antony and Lepidus, and proposed the formation of a new triumvirate. About their fateful meeting, Appian writes:

> Octavian and Antony composed their differences on a small . . . islet in the Lavinius River [in northern Italy]. . . .

Each had five legions of soldiers whom they stationed opposite each other. . . . Lepidus by himself went before them, searched the island, and waved his military cloak as a signal to them to come. . . . There the three sat together in council, Octavian in the center because he was consul. They were in conference from morning till night for two days, and came to these decisions . . . that a new magistracy [ruling body, in this case the Second Triumvirate] for settling the civil dissensions should be created by law [unlike the First Triumvirate, which was unofficial and illegal], which Lepidus, Antony, and Octavian should hold [control over] for five years with consular power . . . that a distribution of the [Roman] provinces should be made, giving Antony the whole of Gaul. . . . Spain was assigned to Lepidus, while Octavian was to have Africa, Sardinia, and Sicily. . . . Only the assignment of the parts beyond the Adriatic [that is, in the east] was postponed, since these were still under the control of Brutus and Cassius, against whom Antony and Octavian were to wage war.[42]

A Thirst for Vengeance

During the deliberations on the island, the new triumvirs did more than divide up Rome's lands and powers. They also agreed on a sinister plan to destroy their main rivals and enemies. Their strategy was not only to eliminate political opposition but also to fill the triumvirs' pockets with funds they needed to pay their armies. The plan was to confiscate the fortunes and valuable estates of the prominent and wealthy Romans they slew. And so, as Sulla had done two generations before, Octavian and his partners now composed a list of "enemies of the state" and put into motion a frightening, bloody purge. "At first," historian John B. Firth explains,

> only seventeen names appeared in the fatal list. But [Rome] was already in a state of wild panic, for the triumvirs had dispatched their executioners in advance, so that they might strike down their victims without warning. Rome was suddenly startled one night to learn that four senators had been slain in the streets and that their murderers were hunting for others. . . . When the triumvirs entered Rome soon after . . . the republicans thought that the blood of the unfortunate sev-

enteen would suffice to slake [appease] their new masters' thirst for vengeance. But . . . a second list, containing a hundred thirty names was published, followed shortly afterwards by a third, containing a hundred and fifty more. . . . New names were constantly added, and for weeks Rome and Italy lived in a state of hideous terror, while bloody work was being carried on and the soldiers were hunting down their victims to destruction.[43]

Not surprisingly, Antony made sure that Cicero's name appeared prominently on the lists of the condemned. Octavian initially objected because the famous senator had been instrumental in his own recent rise to power in Rome. And it is probable that the young man genuinely admired Cicero. Many years later, secure in his power as Augustus, Octavian would remember him fondly as a great man and lover of his country. But the twenty-year-old Octavian was less secure, less nostalgic, and decidedly more ruthless. He and Lepidus eventually consented to Antony's demand for Cicero's death on the grounds that the most respected Roman senator symbolized the power and spirit of the Republic the triumvirs wanted to dominate.

Learning of the danger, Cicero fled to his country house at Astura, on the seacoast about fifty miles south of Rome, hoping to catch a boat there for Greece. But he was not fast enough. In his *Life of Cicero*, Plutarch records how Antony's henchmen caught up with the Republic's last great defender:

> The murderers had arrived [at Cicero's villa]. These were the centurion Herennius and Popillius, an officer of the army, who had in the past been

Soldiers of the Roman Legions

In this excerpt from his Histories, *the Greek historian Polybius explains the breakdown of different kinds of soldiers in a typical Roman legion of his day.*

"The tribunes in Rome, after administering the oath [of military service] fix for each legion a day and place at which the men are to present themselves without arms, and then dismiss them. When they come to the rendezvous, they choose the youngest and poorest to form the *velites*; those next to them [in age] are made *hastati*; those in the prime of life *principes*; and the oldest of all *triarii*, those being the names among the Romans of the four classes in each legion distinct in age and equipment. They divide them [in each legion] so that the senior men known as *triarii* number 600, the *principes* 1,200, the *hastati* 1,200, the rest, consisting of the youngest, being *velites*. . . . [The] *velites* are ordered to carry a sword, light javelins, and a light shield. . . . They also wear a plain helmet, and sometimes cover it with a wolf's skin . . . to protect it and to act as a distinguishing mark by which their officers can recognize them. . . . The next older group, called *hastati*, are ordered to wear a complete panoply [armored protection consisting of a breastplate, helmet, greaves, and shield]. . . . Besides the shield they also carry a sword. This is excellent for thrusting, and both of its edges cut effectively, as the blade is very strong and firm. In addition, they have two heavy javelins (*pila*). . . . The *principes* and *triarii* are armed in the same manner except that instead of *pila* the *triarii* carry long spears."

The Roman soldier at left wears a lorca squamata, *a tunic of armor scales, and holds a* cornu, *a curved battle trumpet; the other man wears a* lorca segmentata, *a leather tunic with attached metal strips.*

A modern drawing depicts the last tragic moments before the death of Cicero (wearing toga). Antony's henchman, Herennius (at left with sword), is about to turn and brutally murder the great orator-statesman.

defended by Cicero when he was prosecuted for having murdered his father. They had their helpers with them. They found the doors shut and broke them down; but Cicero was not to be seen and the people in the house said that they did not know where he was. Then . . . a young man . . . Philologus by name, told the officer that the litter [on which Cicero was riding] was being carried down to the sea by a path that was under the cover of the trees. The officer took a few men with him and hurried round to the place where the path came out of the woods, and Herennius went running down the path. Cicero heard him coming and ordered his servants to set the litter down where they were. He himself, in that characteristic posture of his, with his chin resting on his left hand, looked steadfastly at his murderers. He was all covered in dust; his hair was long and disordered, and his face was pinched and wasted with his anxieties—so that most of those who stood by covered their faces while Herennius was killing him. His throat was cut as he stretched his neck out from the litter. He was in his sixty-fourth year.[44]

As an example, and also for spite, Antony ordered Cicero's head and hands cut off and nailed to a platform in the Roman

Forum. Then, in full public view, Antony's wife, with a triumphant laugh, pierced the dead man's tongue with her dress pin. Many onlookers bemoaned the fact that the lust for power by a handful of men had sunk a great and civilized people to such low levels of cruelty and barbarism.[45]

Deciding Rome's Fate

But the demise of Cicero and the triumvirs' other rivals in Italy was not enough to ensure the triumvirate total power. By the summer of 42 B.C., Brutus and Cassius had managed to raise more than eighty thousand troops still loyal to the Republic, and these forces waited in Greece to fight those of the triumvirs. The inevitable showdown took the form of two pitched battles, separated by an interval of three weeks, on the plain of Philippi in northern Greece in October 42. According to Appian, as the ranks of the opposing forces faced each other in the decisive second encounter, all involved knew that the fate of the Republic was at stake.

> [The soldiers] did not now remember that they were fellow-citizens of their enemies, but hurled threats at each other as though they had been enemies by birth and descent, so much did the anger of the moment extinguish reason and nature in them. Both sides divined [realized] equally that this day and this battle would decide the fate of Rome completely; and so indeed it did.[46]

The struggle at Philippi, which Appian later described as "superb and terrible," was a drawn-out and bloody affair. In the end, Antony and Octavian's forces won, leaving the former conspirators hopeless and humiliated; rather than surrender, Brutus and Cassius committed suicide by falling on their swords and the last credible chance of restoring the Republic died with them.

For many of the defeated Romans, the aftermath of the battle proved just as terrible. Later, in the *Res gestae*, Octavian would record the victory simply and matter-of-factly, stating, "I drove into exile . . . the men who butchered my parent [Caesar] and avenged their crime; later, when they

This famous statue of Augustus Caesar (formerly Octavian), found at Prima Porta, near Rome, shows him wearing a general's breastplate with embossed decorations.

Victory at Philippi

Winning the struggle at Philippi in 42 B.C. left the members of the Second Triumvirate supreme in the Roman world. This synopsis of the basic strategies and tactics of the opposing sides is by military historian Lawrence Keppie (from his article in Warfare in the Ancient World*).*

"Leaving Lepidus to control Italy, Antony and Octavian crossed the Adriatic to Dyrrhachium [in northern Greece] and from there marched eastwards along a main Roman highway, the Via Egnatia, until they encountered their opponents' forces sitting astride the road at the town of Philippi, some 120 km [74 miles] north-east of Thessaloniki. Both armies contained some 19 legions. The army of the Liberators [republicans] was superior in cavalry, and contained some Syrian horse-archers, but they were never able to deploy them. Both sides entrenched [dug in], building stone dikes, palisades [defensive walls], and towers. At first, Brutus and Cassius declined battle, and the resourceful Antony attempted an outflanking movement [marching around and behind the enemy]. . . . Cassius [having detected Antony's move] built a counter-fortification, and intercepted Antony's troops. This led to a general battle, in which Octavian's wing was beaten by Brutus, and Cassius's by Antony. Cassius over-hastily took his own life. There was now a long lull (three weeks rather than Shakespeare's two hours) during which the Caesarians [triumvirs] continued to change the angle of attack, employing their forces in a potentially dangerous maneuver along the edge of [a] marsh. Brutus extended [and thereby thinned] his lines eastwards to avoid being outflanked. Finally, Brutus agreed to a battle, against his better judgment. His troops were forced back and their lines broke up. Victory [for Antony] was complete."

made war on the state, I defeated them twice in pitched battle."[47] This assessment was purposely distorted or misleading in three ways. First, the senators had not been making war on the state; rather, they themselves represented the state, which

the triumvirs had taken control of by force. Second, in point of fact Octavian had not, per his claim, defeated the conspirators. Militarily speaking, Antony had been mainly responsible for the victory, while Octavian, ill at the time, had sat out most of the fighting. And third, so as not to tarnish his own noble image, Octavian failed to mention in the *Res gestae* his own shameful conduct in the days following the battle. According to Suetonius, Octavian, who was caught up in the bloodlust of the times,

> showed no clemency to his beaten enemies, but sent Brutus's head to Rome for throwing at the feet of Caesar's divine image; and insulted the more distinguished of his prisoners. When one of them humbly asked for the right of decent burial, he got the cold answer: "That must be settled with the vultures." And when a father and son pleaded for their lives, Octavian, it is said, told them to decide which of the two should be spared, by casting lots. . . . The father sacrificed his life for the son, and was executed; the son then committed suicide; Octavian watched them both die. His conduct so disgusted the remainder of the prisoners . . . that while being led off in chains they courteously saluted Antony . . . but abused Octavian to his face with the most obscene curses.[48]

By such deeds and conduct, Octavian, like Caesar and others before him, made himself a feared and hated figure in order to acquire and hold on to power. Indeed, as the year 42 drew to a close, he and the other triumvirs enjoyed complete mastery of the Roman sphere. But that mastery could only be maintained if the three men could continue to work together. The lessons of recent Roman history suggested that the odds were greatly against them.

4 Prophecies and Propaganda: The World Divided into Opposing Camps

The dust from the bloody plain of Philippi had barely settled when the power struggle among the members of the Second Triumvirate began. Having defeated the senatorial forces, the first order of business for Antony, Octavian, and Lepidus was to divide up the Mediterranean world among themselves. They all agreed that Italy, the Roman heartland, should remain common territory, to be ruled by the triumvirate as a whole.

However, each man desperately wanted and bargained hard for authority over the largest and choicest of Rome's other territorial possessions. The results of their wheeling and dealing left Octavian with Spain and the large island of Sardinia, off Italy's western coast, and Lepidus in charge of northern Africa, formerly the Carthaginian homeland. Since Antony, as the principal victor at Philippi, was considered the dominant partner in the triumvirate, he received the best share of all—what was known as the "east." This region consisted of the Roman provinces in Greece, Asia Minor, and the Near East. Whoever controlled the area would also have much authority and influence over a number of weak independent eastern kingdoms such as Egypt.[49]

Indeed, command of the east gave Antony some important advantages over the other triumvirs. First, the east was the richest section of the Mediterranean world, boasting great trading centers such as Alexandria in Egypt and Antioch in Syria. Second, Roman forces in the eastern sphere were large and well organized. In addition to strong war fleets, Antony gained control of about eight legions, each containing about five thousand troops, and some ten thousand cavalry. By contrast, Octavian had only three legions and perhaps four thousand horsemen under his own command.

If the triumvirs had not been ambitious and ruthless men, such differences in territory, riches, and military power might not have mattered. However, they *were* ambitious and ruthless; therefore, they quickly became jealous and suspicious of one other, each hoping that sooner or later he would get some or all of his partners' bounty. In the nine years following Philippi, the triumvirs would increasingly employ intrigues, name-calling, and eventually overt threats, until their partnership was in tatters and the Roman world was poised once again on the brink of a ruinous civil war.

Leveling the Playing Field

The first indication that the triumvirate was in trouble was that soon after the three men divided up the empire Lepidus found himself unhappy with his portion. Clearly, the African province was large and fertile. But it contained no major cities and held little strategic importance. On the other hand, Antony had the wealth and military forces of the east. And although Italy, including the strategically important island of Sicily, was supposed to be neutral territory for the triumvirs, Octavian had taken firm charge of the region. Seeing that his partners had managed to push him into a subordinate position, the disgruntled Lepidus eventually decided to act. According to Henry Rowell, in the autumn of 36 B.C. Lepidus

> laid claim to Sicily . . . and ordered Octavian . . . to evacuate it. In doing so, he vastly overestimated his own qualities of leadership, misjudged the temper of his [own] army, and ignored one of his opponent's most powerful weapons—his proven ability to win over the minds and hearts of soldiers. Octavian addressed himself to this weapon with skill and courage. He not only sent agitators among Lepidus's troops, but, in an act of bravery which almost cost him his life, he rode into Lepidus's camp to persuade his soldiers to defect. He knew that they were sick of fighting and that Lepidus enjoyed little popularity among his . . . troops. The risk was well calculated. Mass defections ensued, and Lepidus, stripped of his military power, was forced to implore [beg for] mercy.[50]

Luckily for Lepidus, Octavian was indeed merciful and granted the other man his life. However, Lepidus lost his place in the triumvirate, along with most of his titles and all of his military authority, and remained under house arrest until his death twenty-four years later.

Even with Lepidus out of the way, the triumvirate's authority still prevailed, for the partnership itself remained a legal entity; in effect, all that had happened was that the power game's playing field had been leveled to include two contestants instead of three. On the surface, the triumvirate appeared to be as strong as ever, for to the average Roman on the street it seemed that Octavian and Antony were congenial colleagues. Only four years before, in October 40, they had signed a document of mutual friendship known as the Treaty of Brundisium. To seal the bargain, Antony, whose first wife Fulvia had recently died, agreed to marry Octavian's recently widowed sister, Octavia. As Plutarch tells it:

> Everybody concurred [agreed] in promoting this alliance [except, of course, for Lepidus], fully expecting that with the beauty, honor and prudence of Octavia . . . all would be kept in the safe and happy course of friendship. So, both parties being agreed, they went to Rome to celebrate . . . the Senate [by Octavian's demand] dispensing with the law by which a widow was not permitted to marry till ten months after the death of her husband.[51]

But the treaty and the marriage did not bring the safety and happiness the parties had hoped for. Not surprisingly, neither Octavian nor Antony really

This European engraving, created more than fifteen centuries after Augustus's time, somewhat fancifully depicts him in full military attire and wearing a victor's laurel wreath on his head.

wanted to share power, and they soon began to search for ways to discredit each other. In this regard, Octavian was fortunate, for Antony's behavior continued to be erratic, reckless, and even scandalous; certainly it was unbefitting of a Roman leader of his high position and authority. According to Plutarch, only months after becoming a triumvir, Antony

> plunged once more into his old life of pleasure and debauchery. His general reputation was bad enough, but he

aroused still more hatred on account of the house in which he lived. It had previously belonged to Pompey the Great, a man who was admired . . . for his sobriety and his modest, orderly, and democratic way of life. . . . People were indignant when they saw that this house was [by Antony] most often barred to generals, magistrates, and ambassadors, who found themselves insolently turned away from the doors, and filled with actors, jugglers, and drunken parasites, upon whom Antony squandered most of the money which he had wrung with such violence and cruelty from his victims.[52]

Antony Bewitched?

To Romans of all classes, Antony's reputation was damaged even more when he, like his former mentor, Caesar, came under the influence of the most powerful and ambitious woman in the world. Antony and Cleopatra's relationship, a union that would one day plunge the Mediterranean world into turmoil, began in the summer of 41 B.C. Eager to get his hands on Egyptian money, ships, and grain, Antony summoned the young queen, a Roman vassal, to his headquarters at Tarsus in southern Asia Minor. Cleopatra wanted Roman protection against some of her neighbors, who posed a potential threat to her kingdom. So she gladly agreed to go to Antony, whom she had briefly met a few years before when he had accompanied Caesar to Egypt. Her grand arrival in her huge and luxurious barge was designed to impress both the Roman leader and the local population, and she certainly succeeded. In his biography of Antony, Plutarch describes this unforgettable spectacle:

> She came sailing up the river Cydnus, in barge with gilded [gold-covered] stern and outspread sails of purple, while oars of silver beat time to the music of flutes and fifes and harps. She herself lay all alone under a canopy of cloth of gold, dressed as Venus [the Roman goddess of love] as seen in

paintings, and beautiful young boys, like painted Cupids, stood on each side to fan her. Her maids were dressed like sea nymphs and graces [minor goddesses], some steering at the rudder, some working at the rigging ropes. The perfumes diffused themselves from the vessel to the shore, which was covered with multitudes [of local people], part following the galley up the river on either bank, part running out of the city to see the sight.[53]

Cleopatra put on an even more lavish show that evening when Antony accepted her dinner invitation. According to Plutarch, the banquet was "magnificent beyond expression" and the Roman desired to return the favor as best as he could. The next night, they dined in his headquarters. But he was embarrassed when both his party and his conversational abilities were clearly no match for hers. Sensing his dilemma, the worldly queen put him at ease by adopting his somewhat crude mannerisms and sense of humor. This gesture won Antony over to her charms, which were said to be considerable. Plutarch sums them up by saying that

> the contact of her presence . . . was irresistible; the attraction of her person, joining with the charm of her conversation, and the character that attended all she said or did, was something bewitching. It was a pleasure merely to hear the sound of her voice, with which, like an instrument of many strings, could pass [easily] from one language to another.[54]

That Antony and most other men found Cleopatra delightful and charming is undoubtedly factual. However, Plutarch's assertion that Cleopatra bewitched men, including Antony, betrayed the historian's Roman prejudice. It is true that during the following several weeks Antony, forty-one, and Cleopatra, twenty-eight, became lovers and political partners. But, as historian Peter Green points out, the two "had highly practical ulterior reasons for cultivating one another." She agreed to supply him with huge amounts of money and grain and in exchange he agreed to protect her against her enemies, both domestic and foreign. "How much personal chemistry helped the equation is hard to tell." [55] In any case, the idea that Antony helped her because her hypnotic spells and smells had robbed him of his common sense is extremely far-fetched. Both Antony and Cleopatra were mature and very ambitious adults who saw the chance to use each other to their own ends and enjoy themselves at the same time. Clearly, they both hoped and expected to reap material as well as sexual gains from the relationship.

Thus, claims such as Plutarch's, or Appian's—that Antony "became her [sexual] captive as though he were a young man" [56]—were biased and surely distorted the truth. To these Roman apologists, as well as most Romans, Cleopatra was a wealthy foreigner to be distrusted and envied. She was also a woman in charge of a country, a highly unusual situation in the ancient world (or the modern world,

This highly detailed nineteenth-century painting shows Cleopatra sailing up the Nile on one of her magnificent pleasure barges.

for that matter) and one that most men of the day found distasteful and suspicious. It is no wonder, then, that most ancient writers depicted Cleopatra as a corrupt and "wicked" character who used men solely for her own gains. Unfortunately, it is this image of the famous queen, who was actually a capable and dedicated ruler, that was passed down through the ages.

Cleopatra's Image

Almost all of the ancient historians, Roman and non-Roman alike, criticized and maligned Cleopatra's character and in the process created her now famous image as a charming but deceitful user of men. Usually, she is depicted both as a seductress and a kind of witch who can weave powerful spells to make men do whatever she wants them to. Perhaps the most often quoted of these negative descriptions is that of Plutarch in his *Life of Antony*, which states, "Her actual beauty, it is said, was not in itself so remarkable . . . but the contact of her presence, if you lived with her, was irresistible; the attraction of her person . . . and the character of all she said or did, was something bewitching."

The historian Appian echoes the same theme, writing in his *Roman History* that Antony "was amazed at her wit as well as her good looks, and became her [sexual] captive as though he were a young man. . . . Whatever Cleopatra ordered was done, regardless of laws, human or divine." The Jewish historian Flavius Josephus is more direct and harsh, accusing her of various crimes in addition to her sexual misadventures. In his *Antiquities of the Jews* he calls her a "wicked creature," who "was a slave to her lusts, but she still imagined that she wanted everything she could think of, and did her utmost to gain it. . . . She was also by nature very greedy, and did not hesitate to do evil deeds. She had already poisoned her brother [a claim still unproven] . . . [and she] would violate both temples and tombs . . . from which she would [steal] sacred objects."

Today, it is clear that many, if not most, of these attacks on Cleopatra's character are unfair. Appian, Josephus, and other writers like them despised the idea of a woman who aspired to equality with men and they sought to discredit the notion by damaging her image. Modern scholars generally see the Egyptian queen as a strong, versatile, and courageous individual, as well as an effective leader.

Rome's First Lady Humiliated

Eventually, Antony left Egypt and returned to Rome. There he concluded the Treaty of Brundisium with Octavian, married Octavia, and pursued his ambitions as before. Between 40 and 37 B.C., therefore, Cleopatra had to live without her most powerful ally. She had ample reason for feeling bitter and abandoned, since he had not only married another woman but also left her pregnant with what turned out to be twins. Just a few weeks after the marriage of Antony and Octavia, Cleopatra gave birth to a boy and girl, whom she named Alexander Helios and Cleopatra Selene.

Yet the young queen showed no bitterness. She kept in periodic touch with Antony by messenger and devoted all of her considerable energies to running her country. This is strong evidence for the theory that Cleopatra understood and accepted that much of her relationship with Antony was political in nature. Evidently she was well aware that he, like herself, sometimes had to pursue certain actions and policies he did not like in order to acquire and maintain power.

But whatever the true nature of Antony and Cleopatra's relationship, all that mattered to Octavian was how it looked to others, especially the Roman people. Few Romans had liked or trusted Cleopatra to begin with, and some had expressed their displeasure at her affair with Antony in Tarsus. In 37 B.C., Antony gave them more to grumble about by abandoning Octavia and returning to Cleopatra.[57] The reunited lovers made themselves a new headquarters in

A fanciful portrait of Cleopatra, the last of the Ptolemies. Her actual appearance is a matter of dispute among scholars.

Athens, Greece; from there Antony coldly sent Octavia a document informing her that he was divorcing her. As John Firth explains:

> This was the crowning insult which he could offer to the first lady of the Roman world, who had done even more than her duty to her infatuated and unworthy husband. Octavian desired his sister to quit Antony's roof [in Rome] and take up her abode with him. But she refused, and still continued to care not only for her own children by Antony, but for the children of Antony and Fulvia. . . . Despite the indignities that had been heaped upon her, she maintained a brave front before the world.[58]

The Loyal and Honorable Octavia

In this excerpt from his Life of Antony (Dryden's translation), Plutarch describes Octavia's steadfast devotion to her husband Antony despite the abuses he had heaped on her.

"When Octavia returned from Athens [where she had been residing temporarily until Antony announced he was divorcing her], Octavian, who felt that she had been treated badly, commanded her to live in a separate house; but she refused to leave the house of her husband, and begged him [her brother] that unless he had already decided to make war on Antony, he should for her sake leave matters as they were; it would be intolerable [she pointed out] to have it said of the two greatest commanders in the world that they had involved the Roman people in a civil war, the one out of passion for, the other out of resentment about, a woman [namely, Cleopatra]. And her behavior proved her words to be sincere. She remained in Antony's house as if he were at home in it, and took the noblest and most generous care, not only of his children by her, but of those by Fulvia [his first wife] also. She received all the friends of Antony who came to Rome to seek office or upon any business, and did her utmost to prefer their requests to Octavian; yet this her honorable behavior did but, without her meaning it, damage the reputation of Antony; the wrong he did to such a woman made him hated."

Octavia, Antony's wife and Octavian's sister, failed to persuade her husband to abandon Cleopatra and return to Rome.

Antony soon added insult to injury by sending agents to Rome and physically evicting Octavia from her home, which further sullied his reputation in the empire's capital.

Octavian's Propaganda Machine

Needless to say, Antony's outrageous behavior and cruelty toward Octavia angered Octavian. From a political standpoint it also played right into his hands. Octavian had been searching for some wedge to drive between Antony and the Roman people, some way to make his rival triumvir look like an unworthy leader and, if possible, even a traitor to his country. So it is hardly surprising that Octavian now began a propaganda campaign in earnest against Antony. In this endeavor Octavian was in his true element, for it was such purely political and verbal warfare, rather than the battlefield variety, that revealed his true talents. "The political gifts of Octavian were of a very high order," Donald Dudley remarks:

> He could appraise a political situation with the cool judgment that Caesar had brought to military affairs. . . . Above all, he had what Caesar lacked, an acute sense of the emotive power of words, titles, and slogans. It was this that made him such a master of propaganda.[59]

As an opening move, Octavian announced publicly that he had acquired a copy of Antony's will. Whether the document was genuine or a clever forgery engineered by Octavian's henchmen will never

be known. In any case, the Roman Senate accepted its authenticity, as did most ordinary Romans. All were duly shocked to discover that Antony desired to be buried not in Italy, as any respectable Roman would, but in Cleopatra's tomb in Alexandria. Even more upsetting, the will supposedly also acknowledged that the earlier union between Cleopatra and Julius Caesar was lawful. That implied that the male offspring of that union, Caesarion, now about eleven years old, was Caesar's legitimate son, and further, that the boy—not Octavian—was the rightful heir to Caesar's titles, lands, and powers.

Octavian made sure these damaging sections of the will were read before the Senate. Here was a sound foundation on which he could build his case that Antony intended to abandon his homeland, just as he had poor Octavia, and make Alexandria the new capital of the Mediterranean world. There was an even darker aspect of the picture Octavian was painting. If Antony succeeded, he suggested, Cleopatra, that "wicked queen and bewitcher and corrupter of decent men," would become the queen of Rome. It was Octavian's deliberate aim, writes Firth, "to array upon his side the pride and jealousy of the Roman people, to exaggerate and paint in the darkest colors the influence and ambition of Cleopatra, to represent that the Roman religion and the Roman civilization were threatened by the alien gods [of the east] and the alien civilization of the Nile."[60]

At this juncture, as unpopular as he was with many Romans, Antony still had at least a chance to redeem himself. Octavia still insisted that she wanted him back, and perhaps leaving Cleopatra and offering heartfelt apologies to his countrymen might have foiled Octavian's scheme. However, Antony continued to commit what his rival called reckless and insulting acts. In January 35 B.C. Cleopatra gave birth to her third child by Antony, a boy named Ptolemy Philadelphus. This looked bad enough in Rome. Then came the news that Octavia was on her way to the east, bringing troops and supplies as an offer of support to her former husband. Clearly choosing between the two women, he sent word to Octavia that her mission was useless and unwanted and ordered her to return to Rome. This marked the great turning point in Antony's career. By firmly siding with Cleopatra, a foreign monarch, against Rome and the Roman institution of marriage, he seemed to be turning his back on his homeland and its cherished values.

In the following two years, Antony continued to tarnish his former image of respectability as a Roman leader; and Octavian, of course, took full advantage of the situation. Rumors filtered back to Rome that Antony was growing increasingly corrupt, wearing Egyptian clothes, and doing the bidding of the notorious Egyptian queen. The later Roman historian Dio Cassius wrote that Cleopatra had

enslaved him so completely that . . . she was saluted by him as "queen" and as "mistress," and she had Roman soldiers [his men] in her bodyguard, all of whom had her name inscribed upon their shields. She visited the market-place with Antony . . . [following] on foot together with her eunuchs [castrated attendants]. He also . . . carried an Oriental [eastern-style] dagger in his belt, wore clothes which were completely alien to Roman cus-

tom, and appeared in public seated upon a gilded couch or chair. Painters and sculptors depicted him with Cleopatra, he being represented as Osiris [Egyptian god of the afterlife] . . . and she as . . . Isis [ruler of heaven

This carving from the Egyptian temple of Dendera purportedly depicts Cleopatra.

and earth], and it was this practice more than anything else which gave the impression that she had laid him under some spell and deprived him of his wits.[61]

It is doubtful that Antony became as subservient as Roman writers depict him. It appears that he was indeed turning his back on his country; but his actions were more likely motivated by his vaunting ambition and thirst for power than by a loss of his wits. Apparently, he believed that with the riches and manpower of the east at his disposal he could eventually sweep Octavian aside and become the sole ruler of Rome. Octavian's propaganda machine certainly spread a continuous stream of rumors to that effect.

A Gaudy and Arrogant Display

That these rumors were far less exaggerated and in fact more ominous than the rest of Octavian's charges became obvious in 34 B.C., when Antony and Cleopatra staged a huge and magnificent public ceremony. Known as the Donations of Alexandria, it was attended by gigantic crowds. And hidden among these excited and curious onlookers were Octavian's agents, who later reported to him in glowing detail what they had witnessed. The following description is Plutarch's summary of the spectacular event, in which Antony granted several eastern Roman territories to his and Cleopatra's children, something he had no legal right to do.

Assembling the people in the exercise ground, and causing two golden thrones to be placed on a platform of silver, the one for him and the other for Cleopatra, and at their feet lower thrones for their children, he proclaimed Cleopatra queen of Egypt, Cyprus, Lybia, and Coele-Syria, and [ruling] with her conjointly Caesarion, the reputed son of the former Caesar. . . . His [Antony's] own sons by Cleopatra were to have the style of king of kings; to Alexander [Helios] he gave Armenia and Media [Persia] . . . to Ptolemy [Philadephus], Phoenicia, Syria, and Cilicia. Alexander was brought out before the people in Median costume . . . and Ptolemy, in boots and mantle [cloak] and Macedonian cap done about with the diadem [crown]; for this was the habit of the successors of Alexander [the Great, whose follower, Ptolemy, had established the Ptolemaic dynasty]. . . . Cleopatra was then, as at other times when she appeared in public, dressed in the habit [outfit] of the goddess Isis, and gave audience to the people under the name of the New Isis.[62]

Back in Italy, reaction to this gaudy and arrogant display was predictable. According to Dio Cassius, the Romans were so outraged that "they were willing to believe other rumors current at the time," among these that Antony "would hand over the city of Rome to Cleopatra and transfer the seat of government to Egypt."[63] In the wake of these charges, in the following months even many of Antony's closest friends and diehard supporters began to turn against him.

By this time, however, Antony and Cleopatra cared little about their public image in faraway Rome. In fact, the Donations ceremony had been a deliberate part of their own propaganda campaign, one that was meant to instill feelings of awe, fear, and solidarity among the peoples of the eastern Mediterranean region. They were, in effect, announcing that this region was already in a sense their own empire, one that could and would stand up against and eventually overshadow the Roman heartland. This tactic was designed to exploit existing anti-Roman sentiment. After all, the idea of challenging and defeating Rome was very appealing to many in the east, who still deeply resented living under the yoke of Roman imperialism.

Manipulating Ancient Prophecy

Antony and Cleopatra soon used propaganda in an even more effective way against Octavian. By manipulating ancient prophecies, they embarrassed their chief rival and at the same time bolstered their own prestige. For centuries, priests and writers in various Mediterranean lands had predicted the coming of a golden age, a new world order in which wars and crime would be eliminated and happy times would prevail. These stories often foretold that a special person, one usually associated in some way with the sun, would emerge to lead the new order. For example, until his untimely death it was widely believed that Alexander the Great was this new leader.

Publius Vergilius Maro, popularly known as Virgil, was one of several Roman writers who dealt with the theme of the coming golden age and the prophesied new leader. In 40 B.C. he had composed his *Fourth Eclogue*, which states in part:

> The Last Age is at hand; the great cycle of ages begins afresh. . . . Down from the high heaven is sent a new progeny [child]. On the Boy soon to be born, who'll end the Race of Iron [the present age] and make the Race of Gold [bathed in the sun's rays] rise up. . . . He'll share the Life of the Gods; Heroes he'll see mingled with Gods, himself beheld by them: he'll rule the peaceful Earth with his father's Virtues.[64]

Virgil's widely popular poem had been intended to help legitimize that year's Treaty of Brundisium, the political deal made by Antony and Octavian, and the coincidental marriage of Antony and Octavia. The poem promoted the idea that the couple's "progeny" would carry the superior blood of the two most powerful triumvirs. This shrewd combination of prophecy and propaganda suggested that the son of Antony and Octavia, who was also Octavian's nephew, would one day rule over a new and better Roman world. Of course, Antony subsequently negated the prophecy by shunning Rome and siding with Cleopatra.

Now, at the height of the propaganda war, Antony and Cleopatra resurrected Virgil's poem and used it to their own advantage. They implied that she, and not Octavia, was the mother of the semidivine boy mentioned in the prophecy. That young Alexander Helios bore the name of another figure who had been associated with the prophecy, Alexander the Great, and also of the Greek sun god, Helios, seemed to confirm this interpretation.

An engraving by George Cooke depicts the bust of Rome's great epic poet, Publius Vergilius Maro, popularly known as Virgil, as a young man.

Antony and Cleopatra made the boy a symbol of the new world they wanted to build in place of the "corrupt" one domi- nated by Rome. And this strategy seemed to pay off. Many eastern peoples, eager for any excuse to oppose Rome, offered to support an anti-Roman crusade led by Antony, Cleopatra, and their "heaven-sent" son.[65]

Thus, by 33 B.C. Rome's empire had polarized into a western camp led by Octavian and an eastern camp led by Antony and Cleopatra. Years of outrageous rhetoric, posturing, and slander from both sides had created a highly volatile atmosphere, a dangerous political climate in which war seemed the only way to reconcile their differences. And so, each camp began to arm itself for the coming struggle. History seemed ready to repeat itself as the ambitions of a few power-hungry individuals threatened to plunge the already war-weary Roman world into another devastating civil war. It was a time of wild and dramatic prophecies, when many claimed the ability to foretell coming events. Yet no one predicted, or in all likelihood even imagined, that the outcome of the new war would be decided in a single great battle.

Chapter

5 The Victor's Wrath and the People's Justice: The Battle of Actium

In 32 B.C. the Roman world was divided. The forces of the east and west began preparing in earnest for an armed confrontation that all involved knew would decide the fate of the Mediterranean sphere, perhaps for generations to come. On one side stood Octavian, now the most powerful man in Rome. With Lepidus under house arrest and Antony in open rebellion against the Roman government, Octavian was the sole remaining triumvir and as such retained all the considerable legal powers of the triumvirate; that meant that he could marshal the many troops and ships of Italy and the western sector of the empire.

Yet Octavian was well aware that the opposition he faced was strong and potentially deadly. Antony and Cleopatra had the loyalty of thousands of Roman troops stationed in the east, as well as promises of troops and ships from numerous eastern kingdoms. And the ships, grain, and especially the money of Egypt were certainly important strategic assets that might turn the tide of war in favor of the infamous lovers. In addition, in spite of Octavian's propaganda campaign, Antony still enjoyed the support of many Roman leaders who for their own reasons did not like or trust Octavian. In the spring of 32, the two consuls, along with nearly three hundred senators—about one-third of the Senate—fled Rome and joined Antony. Thus, each side had reason to believe that it could prevail over the other in the coming fight and end up ruling a reunited Roman world.

Assembling the Forces

In fact, Antony's and Cleopatra's resources, both real and potential, seemed to them so vast that they became overconfident; in the long run, this may have cost them the war. Early in 32 B.C., Octavian found his own war preparations stalled by widespread protests in Italy. In order to raise and outfit the troops he needed for the coming struggle, he had had no choice but to increase taxes sharply and many disgruntled Romans had been slow to pay. Some refused to pay at all and staged public demonstrations. According to Plutarch, "Full citizens were obliged to pay over one quarter of the income and freedmen one eighth of their property, with the result that there was a violent outcry from both classes against Octavian and disturbances broke out all over Italy."[66]

This should have been Antony's cue to take the initiative and attack Italy while his foe was unprepared. But instead, Antony took his time assembling his forces. He leisurely traveled with Cleopatra to Greece, where the two staged elaborate festivals and ceremonies designed to advertise their power and prestige. This gave Octavian the time he needed to put down the tax protests and outfit his own forces. As Plutarch puts it, Antony's failure to act on his advantage

> is now considered to have been one of his greatest errors of judgment, since it gave Octavian the opportunity to complete his preparations and allowed time for the indignation aroused by his [tax] measures [in Italy] to subside. People felt rebellious at the moment when the money was extorted from them, but, once they had paid it, their anger cooled off.[67]

Octavian put his able commander Marcus Vipsanius Agrippa in charge of his war preparations. Though only about thirty at the time, Agrippa had distinguished himself as a first-rate general/admiral by defeating a force of dangerous rebels in Sicily four years before. The new fleet of warships he had built for that operation now proved to be a fortunate boon for Octavian's campaign against Antony. These vessels were mostly triremes, lightweight and very maneuverable ships with three banks of oars on each side. According to Plutarch, Agrippa had about 250 such warships; other ancient historians maintain that he had closer to 400. Both figures may have merit, for the second may represent the total of war galleys plus the necessary supporting supply ships and troop transports. Agrippa also had about eighty thousand land troops at his disposal.

In contrast, Antony commanded a considerably larger host. His land forces included 19 Roman legions—about 60,000 to 65,000 tough, well-trained heavy infantrymen—and another 70,000 to 75,000 light-armed troops supplied by his eastern allies. His naval squadrons totaled perhaps 500 or more ships, with crews totaling between 125,000 and 150,000 sailors and fighters. Though these numbers might at first glance seem to give Antony

A bust of Marcus Agrippa, Octavian's friend, military strategist, and personal adviser, who engineered the victory at Actium.

Roman Warships

In the long interval between the Punic Wars in the third century B.C. and the Battle of Actium in 31 B.C., the Romans fought only a few minor naval engagements. However, so as not to be caught off guard in an emergency, during these centuries they maintained a moderately large force of warships. These vessels were of many types. The smallest were biremes, with two banks of oars, and probably carried fewer than 100 men, including rowers. The largest practical warships were quinqueremes, which had five rowers on each oar (or five banks of oars; scholars remain unsure). These vessels often carried crews of up to 300 rowers and sailors and 80 to 120 troops. Mammoth ships having six, eight, or ten banks of oars, like those Antony employed at Actium, were unusual in Roman navies and more common in the eastern kingdoms that supported him in the war.

By far the most common Roman warship of the period, and the vessel that made up most of Agrippa's fleet at Actium, was the trireme. As its name suggests, this ship had three banks of oars, making it faster than a bireme and at the same time lighter and more maneuverable than a quinquereme. Such ships, according to scholars Lesley and Roy Adkins (in *Handbook to Life in Ancient Rome*), "are not known to have exceeded 60 meters (200 feet) in length and were usually far less. They did not stand high above the water and were not very seaworthy or stable, although they were broader and sturdier than earlier Greek ships." Each trireme probably carried a crew of about 220, including perhaps 80 soldiers. Adding the hull, decks, mast, oars, men, weapons, and supplies, such a vessel would have weighed, or in nautical terms displaced, eighty to ninety tons. Yet it was relatively quick for its time. In short spurts, when attacking for instance, it could attain a speed of perhaps seven to eight knots (eight to nine miles per hour).

A war trireme, carrying a full crew and a large detachment of soldiers, makes its way through choppy waters. Most of Agrippa's ships were triremes.

an overwhelming advantage, it is important to consider the types of ships that composed the bulk of his navy. As military historian W. L. Rodgers explains in *Greek and Roman Naval Warfare*:

> The vessels were high and large compared to their adversaries. . . . A few were tetreres [or quadriremes, having four banks of oars] and a few were deceres [with ten banks of oars]. The others were intermediate in size [with five, six, or eight banks of oars]. They carried high towers of several stories bearing heavy mechanical artillery [catapults and spear-shooting devices] and the archers. They relied on grappling irons [to snag enemy ships] and a boarders' fight.[68]

This meant that Antony's ships were on the whole much larger, and thus slower and less maneuverable, than Agrippa's. This difference would prove to have great strategic importance when the fleets eventually clashed. Rodgers also makes the point that the crafty Agrippa planned partially to make up for his inferior numbers and smaller ships by using special offensive weapons of his own design.

> Now [that] they had to win against ships bigger than themselves . . . Agrippa prepared to turn the scale by the provision of new devices for throwing fire. I do not mean to say that fire-throwing was previously unknown, for . . . it was used . . . in the campaign of Philippi, but Romans had been accustomed to win at sea against inferior soldiers by the exertions of hard-fighting legionaries on the ships' decks. Here would be legionaries on both sides and Agrippa was preparing

a tactical surprise. Contrary to Roman practice, he was going to make a principal effort against ship structure instead of relying chiefly on infantry.[69]

Octavian Seizes the Initiative

Whatever his material advantages or disadvantages may have been, Octavian seized the tactical advantage by taking the initiative. Instead of waiting in Italy for the enemy to come to him, early in 31 B.C. he began advancing on Greece. He had already publicly denounced Antony as a traitor and a rebel and formally declared war on Cleopatra. Leaving Antony's name out of the war declaration was Octavian's attempt to make the struggle look like a war against a foreign aggressor rather than a civil war, which of course it was. Apparently he hoped this gesture would instill some sense of purpose and confidence in his troops, who faced the unsavory task of fighting their fellow Romans.

To boost the confidence of his troops still further, Octavian took full advantage of the prevailing belief in omens, supposed supernatural signs foretelling the outcome of ensuing events. According to his propaganda, which Plutarch later duly recorded:

> These omens are said to have announced the war: Pisaurum, where Antony had settled a colony on the Adriatic Sea, was swallowed up by an earthquake; sweat ran from one of the marble statues of Antony . . . for many days together, and though frequently wiped off, did not stop. When he himself was in the city of Patrae,

the temple of Hercules [a mythical hero from whom Antony claimed he was descended] was struck by lightning. . . . And in Cleopatra's admiral-galley, which was called the Antonias, a most unfavorable omen occurred. Some swallows had nested in the stern of the galley, but other swallows came, beat the first away, and destroyed their nests.[70]

Factual or not, these widely reported omens seemed to many to bode ill for Antony and Cleopatra's forces. Interpreting the signs as overwhelmingly favorable for their own forces, Octavian and Agrippa advanced into Greece while their adversaries' army and navy were still disorganized and unprepared. In March 31, Agrippa boldly captured the port of Methone, on Greece's southern coast, one of Antony's vital naval bases. From there, Agrippa's warships raided other ports in the region and seriously disrupted Antony's supply lines. At the same time, Octavian marched his land troops down Greece's western coast and established a large camp near Actium, at the mouth of the wide Ambracian Gulf.

Caught off guard by their opponents' bold moves, Antony and Cleopatra hastily gathered most of their forces and encamped them a mere five miles from Octavian's camp. The lovers evidently thought that their supply line, which extended southward across the Gulf of Corinth in central Greece, was secure. They certainly did not reckon on Agrippa's brilliance as a war strategist, for he quickly executed a series of naval raids and maneuvers that completely shut off his opponents' supply line, thereby trapping their forces in the vicinity of Actium.

Greece in 31 B.C.

Whatever their initial strategy might have been, Antony and Cleopatra now had no choice but to fight.

The question the lovers now faced was whether to engage Octavian's forces on land or at sea. An argument ensued in which Canidius Crassus, Antony's second in command, forcefully made a case for abandoning the fleet and attacking Octavian on land. Crassus, writes Plutarch,

advised Antony to send Cleopatra away, withdraw his troops into Thrace or Macedonia, and trust to a land battle to decide the issue. . . . There would be no disgrace, Canidius urged, in giving up the control of the sea to Octavian, since his forces had been trained in naval operations during [Agrippa's recent campaigns in the west]. . . . On the other hand, it would be absurd for Antony, who was as experienced in fighting on land as any commander living, not to take advantage of the superior numbers and equipment of his legions, but to distribute his fighting men among the ships and so fritter away his strength.[71]

At first, Antony agreed with his officer. But then Cleopatra joined the argument and just as forcefully called for a naval battle. That Antony soon decided in her favor later helped to strengthen the conviction of ancient writers like Plutarch that Antony was under her spell and therefore helpless to refuse her every whim. In reality, Antony realized that his forces were trapped and that without fresh supplies they could not long maintain fighting readiness. It became clear that Octavian and Agrippa, appreciating their enemy's

A highly fanciful nineteenth-century depiction of Antony and Cleopatra during the Battle of Actium. In reality, they commanded separate ships and did not rejoin each other until well after fleeing the conflict.

predicament, intended to keep their distance and refuse a land fight. That left Antony with only one option—to use his ships to try to break out of the trap.

The Commanders Boost Morale

The battle that would decide the fate of tens of millions in the Mediterranean world took place on September 2, 31 B.C. In the morning, the opposing land armies, hoping to watch the coming struggle, marched onto the beaches on either side of the gulf. But the struggle was delayed because there was no wind. All of the warships had oars, of course; but most of the vessels were too large or too weighed down with troops and weapons to move fast or maneuver well without an assist from the sails.

While waiting for the wind to pick up, the commanders on both sides mingled with contingents of their troops, partly to help build up morale. Plutarch writes that "Antony in a small boat went from one ship to another, encouraging his soldiers, and bidding them stand firm and fight as steadily on their large ships as if they were on land." [72] And Dio Cassius offers the following paraphrase of Antony's morale-building speech:

> Soldiers, all the preparations for the war which it is my duty to undertake have been completed in good time. You belong to an army whose strength is as overwhelming as its quality is unsurpassed. . . . Your training has given you such a mastery of every form of combat that is known in our times that each of you, man for man, can strike fear into our adversaries. You can see for yourselves the size and excellence of our fleet and the superiority of our infantry, cavalry, slingers, targeteers and archers. . . . Most of these special troops the enemy do not possess at all, and those that they have are fewer and less well equipped than ours. . . . We shall not be fighting for any petty or trifling stakes. If we are resolute, we shall win the greatest prizes of all; if we are careless, we shall suffer the worst of misfortunes. [73]

On similar rounds, Octavian (according to Dio) told his own troops:

> Soldiers, there is a conclusion I have reached . . . and I urge you to keep it before you. This is that in all the greatest enterprises of war, or indeed in human affairs of any kind, victory comes to those whose thoughts and deeds follow the path of justice and reverence for the gods. . . . We Romans are the rulers of the greatest and best parts of the world, and yet we find ourselves spurned and trampled upon by a woman of Egypt. . . . Who would not tear his hair at the sight of Roman soldiers serving as bodyguards of this queen? Who would not groan at hearing that Roman knights and senators grovel before her? . . . Who would not weep when he sees and hears what Antony has become? . . . He has abandoned his whole ancestral way of life [and] embraced alien and barbaric customs. . . . I cannot describe to you any greater prize than that of upholding the renown which your forefathers won, of preserving the proud tradition of your native land, of punishing those

In his Roman History*, Dio Cassius records that shortly before the battle at Actium Octavian gave his men a morale-boosting speech. Supposedly, Octavian told his sailors:*

"You must not imagine that the size of their ships or the stoutness of their timbers is any match for our courage. . . . I believe that their height and their solid construction will make them more difficult for their rowers to keep under way, and less responsive for their helmsmen to steer. . . . If their ships remain motionless, as if they were moored there, we can rip them open without rams, or else bombard them from a distance with our siege engines [catapults], or burn them to the water's edge with our flaming missiles. . . . Their weight makes them too cumbersome to do damage to us, and their size makes them most liable to suffer it themselves."

who have rebelled against us, of conquering and ruling over all mankind![74]

Also during his rounds, Octavian had an unexpected encounter with a local farmer who was crossing the beach with his donkey. When Octavian asked the man his name, the fellow replied that his nickname was "Fortunate" and that his donkey was called "Conqueror." The Roman leader immediately took these names as a favorable omen sent by the gods, a clear sign that victory would be his. After finishing his inspection of the ships, Octavian, filled with confidence, joined Agrippa in their command vessel and waited for the all-important wind.

The Sound of the Trumpet

They did not have to wait long. In the early afternoon the breezes on the Greek coast began to pick up and the fighting at last commenced. According to Dio Cassius, who based his description on eyewitness accounts:

At the sound of the trumpet Antony's fleet began to move, and, keeping close together, formed their line a little way outside the strait [leading out of the gulf], but then advanced no further. Octavian moved out, as if to engage [the enemy]. . . . But when they neither came out against him, nor turned away . . . Octavian halted his advance, being in doubt as to what to do. He ordered his rowers to let their oars rest in the water, and waited for a while; after this he suddenly made a signal and, advancing both his wings [contingents on the far left and right], rounded his line in the form of an enveloping crescent. His object was to encircle the enemy if possible or, if not, at least to break up their formation. Antony was alarmed by this outflanking and encircling maneuver, moved forward to meet it as best he could, and so unwillingly joined battle with Octavian.[75]

As the struggle began, the men in both fleets raised loud war cries and the armies on the beaches also began shouting encouragements to their respective sea forces. Those onshore watched as Antony wisely increased the distance between his ships, lengthening his front line from perhaps five thousand to eight thousand yards or more. This thwarted Octavian's attempt to encircle his fleet and the two armadas met head on in a crash of splintering oars and showers of arrows, spears, and rocks.

Within a few minutes, the battle tactics of the opposing sides, dictated by the differing sizes of the ships, became readily apparent to all. Octavian and Agrippa's smaller and faster ships attempted to build up bursts of speed and ram the larger, less mobile enemy vessels. The

This artist's conception of a scene from the Battle of Actium correctly shows soldiers on shore (left) cheering their comrades on the ships.

bronze beaks, or rams, on the prows of the triremes were located near the water line, so that when they penetrated the hull of an enemy ship water immediately began to pour into the newly opened breach. As the injured vessel began to take on water, two things happened at once. First, the boat listed, or tilted off balance—forward, backward, or to the side—effectively robbing it of its ability to maneuver. Second, the crew, especially the rowers in the lower decks nearest the rising water, usually panicked, creating chaos onboard and further destroying the vessel's effectiveness. In the meantime, after its successful ramming run, the trireme "back-watered," or rowed furiously backward to free itself from the stricken vessel, and proceeded to attack another enemy ship.

By contrast, the tactics of Antony's ships were mainly to shoot volleys of arrows, stones, and other missiles at the enemy triremes as they approached in their ramming runs. Sometimes these volleys were on target and succeeded in destroying a ship's mast and sail or a bank of its oars, in which case the ramming was avoided. If the missiles missed or did minimal damage, however, the larger vessel could not outrun the attacking ship or ships and a successful ramming was almost certain.

With these tactics, the engagement soon came to resemble a land battle. As Dio Cassius puts it:

Octavian's ships resembled cavalry, now launching a charge, and now retreating, since they could attack or draw off as they chose, while Antony's were like heavy infantry, warding off the enemy's efforts to ram them, but also striving to hold them with their grappling-hooks. Each fleet in turn gained the advantage over the other: the one would dart in against the rows of oars which projected from the ships' sides and break the blades, while the other, fighting from its higher decks, would sink its adversaries with stones and ballistic missiles.[76]

Corroborating Dio is Plutarch, who also states that

the engagement resembled a land fight, or, to speak yet more properly, the attack and defense of a fortified place; for there were always three or four vessels of Octavian's around one of Antony's, pressing them with spears, javelins, poles, and several burning missiles, which they flung among them, Antony's men using catapults also to pour down missiles from wooden towers.[77]

Breaking Out of the Trap

For a while—perhaps two hours or so— the battle raged with neither side gaining a clear upper hand. Then Cleopatra made a move that instantly changed the face of the struggle. With a squadron of about sixty ships, she had maintained a position in the rear of Antony's fleet, and it is unlikely that she had actually been involved thus far in the fighting. It appears that part of her and her lover's plan was for her ships to stay out of the action and guard their flagship. This vessel carried a vast cache of gold and jewels, a treasure they sorely needed to carry on the war.

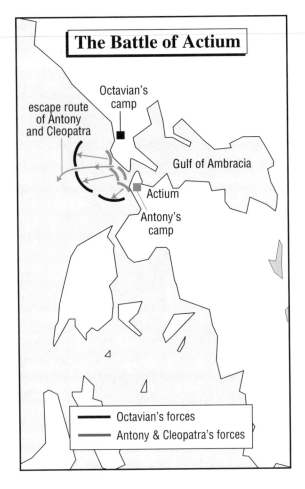

The Battle of Actium

escape route of Antony and Cleopatra

Octavian's camp

Gulf of Ambracia

Actium

Antony's camp

Octavian's forces
Antony & Cleopatra's forces

Interpreting this move as a retreat, Antony abruptly abandoned the fray himself and followed his lover into the open sea. Before he left, he ordered his remaining ships to cover the retreat by staying to fight Octavian's forces.

Most of the soldiers on both sides assumed that Cleopatra was a coward and that Antony, still enslaved by her charms, had coldly left his own men behind to die. Plutarch summarizes this view:

> Here it was that Antony showed to all the world that he was no longer motivated by the thoughts and motives of a commander or a man, or indeed by his own judgment at all . . . for, as if he had been born a part of her, and must move with her wherever she went, as soon as he saw her ship sailing away, he abandoned all that were fighting and spending their lives for him.[79]

But this view was probably shortsighted and distorted by the hatreds and biases the Romans held for Cleopatra. Some modern historians contend that in hoisting sails and charging through the enemy lines the queen was actually launching a courageous and desperate attack on her opponents. Her ships were certainly much too heavy to attack using oar power alone, so they would have had to use their sails.

Even if this theory is incorrect, it is very likely that the lovers had planned their escape from the beginning. The main priority, after all, had been to break out of the trap at Actium; and it is unlikely that they would have risked allowing their treasure to sink to the sea bottom, or worse, to fall into Octavian's hands. Without these riches, they had little chance of fighting other battles and thereby of winning the war. As Ernle Bradford states in

Suddenly, at the height of the battle, the Egyptian queen ordered her vessels to leave their position. Plutarch writes:

> Cleopatra's squadron of sixty ships was suddenly seen to hoist sail and make off through the very midst of the battle. They had been stationed astern of the heavy ships, and so threw their whole formation into disorder as they plunged through. The enemy watched them with amazement, as they spread their sails before the following wind and shaped their course for the Peloponnesus [the southernmost region of Greece].[78]

his biography of Cleopatra, "The romantic version as projected first by Plutarch . . . is clearly not true. . . . Antony's conduct can hardly be considered very noble, but it was practical. He had lost the battle of Actium . . . but he still had a chance to fight another day."[80]

The Tide of Battle Turns

Whatever the reason for Antony and Cleopatra's escape, the move threw their remaining forces into disarray. Antony's men fought on, often valiantly, but without

Ancient Naval Tactics

The idea of winning a war using warships alone was alien to most ancient commanders. The basic strategy behind most ancient naval warfare was to use the fleets to supplement the land armies. As noted military historian John Keegan points out in *A History of Warfare*, "Galley navies were never autonomous [independent] instruments of strategy but [instead] extensions . . . of armies on land. . . . The fleet maneuvered so as to isolate an enemy coastal base . . . while the army advanced with supplies to positions from which the galleys could be reprovisioned."

Thus, warships were not usually built for long voyages and only rarely ventured out of sight of land. They also often fought, as did the ships at Actium, using tactics similar to those employed in land battles. The aim was to engage and destroy the enemy at close quarters, using hand-to-hand combat if possible. In his book *Greek and Roman Naval Warfare*, military scholar W. L. Rodgers writes:

> Until the invention of ship armor and very heavy artillery [in modern times], the attack on personnel [people] was, on the whole, more effective than the attack on ship structure. As long as weapons had only human strength with which to strike . . . weapons were more effective when directed against men than against ships. . . . In general, fleets wished to approach each other for a hand-to-hand struggle, and at the same time they wished to protect their oars on which their mobility depended. . . . Individual ships . . . maneuvered about each other for advantage in bringing about collision [ramming]. . . . The fighting men were armed and equipped after the fashion of soldiers of their own countries and the crews of every pair of opposing ships sought to get positions of advantage for the style of hand-to-hand fighting suited to their own national infantry.

The chaos and destruction of the sea fight at Actium are captured in this drawing. With Agrippa's aid, Octavian won a decisive victory.

a leader they felt the tide of battle steadily turn against them. According to Dio, the struggle "was carried on with the greatest ferocity. Octavian's soldiers battered the lower parts of [Antony's] ships from stem to stern, smashed the oars, broke off the rudders, and, climbing on to the decks, grappled with their enemies."[81]

Eventually, Octavian ordered an all-out assault with Agrippa's new version of "blazing missiles," which set Antony's huge galleys afire. The crews desperately tried to put these blazes out but were uniformly unsuccessful. Dio's riveting account captures the gruesome results:

Some, especially the sailors, were overcome by the smoke before the flames ever came near them, while others were roasted in the midst of the holocaust as if they were in ovens. Others were incinerated [burned to ashes] in their armor as it grew red-hot. Others, again, to avoid such a fate, or when they were half burned, threw off their armor and were wounded by the missiles shot at them from long range, or jumped into the sea and were drowned, or were clubbed by their enemies and sank, or were devoured by sea-monsters [sharks].[82]

The extent of the casualties inflicted and suffered by both sides in the mighty battle remains unknown. What is certain is that Antony's forces were shattered. During the next several days, some of the pitiful survivors of his navy surrendered to Octavian's triumphant troops, while others slipped away and returned in disgrace to their homes.

With Antony soundly defeated, Julius Caesar's great-nephew finally could boast of a military win to match some of the legendary victories of his illustrious ancestor.

To commemorate his success, he had statues of the peasant called Fortunate and his donkey, Conqueror, erected on the exact spot where he had met them. But Octavian did not feel that his great victory was yet complete. Antony and his foreign queen had escaped both the victor's wrath and the justice demanded by the Roman people. Octavian had no choice but to pursue his enemies to Egypt, for he could not effectively rule the empire he had fought so hard to win until he had vented that wrath and exacted that justice.

Chapter
6 Republic Gives Way to Empire: The Lesson of Absolute Power

Octavian's victory at Actium left him, at age thirty-two, the most powerful political figure in a reunited Roman world. But this world was very different from the one in which he and most other Romans had grown up. The long and devastating series of civil wars that had culminated in the bloody waters at Actium had left Rome's republican government in ruins. Cicero, Brutus, and the other champions of the old politics were in their graves and the remaining senators and other high government officials cowered before the vast military array that Octavian now commanded. The way now seemed clear for one overwhelmingly powerful leader to rule the empire virtually unopposed.

In a way, such an arrangement was a simple, if brutal, solution to the fundamental problem the Republic had faced in its last century; namely, how to reconcile the people's will with the wills of ambitious military strongmen. How could representative government and an army loyal to only one man coexist in harmony? Julius Caesar's answer to this question had been that they could *not* coexist, and so he had overpowered the Senate and declared himself dictator for life. But Caesar eventually had paid the ultimate price for his ambition and arrogance, and the battle

between the government and the strongmen had raged on. Shortly after Caesar's murder, one of his friends, Gaius Matius, had written to Cicero, "If Caesar, with all his genius, could not find a way out, who is likely to do so?"[83]

Less than two decades later, Caesar's heir answered Matius's question. Octavian's "way out" of the dilemma of who should rule Rome and how he should go about it was to modify Caesar's approach. Octavian became as absolute a dictator as his father, and more so; but unlike Caesar, he did not rudely run roughshod over the old republican institutions. Octavian acted under the guise of restoring the old government and respecting its principles.

What Octavian actually restored, of course, was the unity of the state and civil order, an act that most Romans greatly appreciated after so many years of chaos, bloodshed, and uncertainty. Indeed, Octavian shrewdly seemed to sense that the Roman people were now ready to accept a single, all-powerful leader, as long as he ruled in an orderly, restrained, and fair manner. In this way, Octavian oversaw the transition from the Roman Republic to the Roman Empire, the mighty political entity that would dominate the Mediterranean world for the next five centuries.

The Dream Unravels

But before Octavian could devote himself to the weighty task of creating a new government, he first had to deal with his principal adversaries, with whom he was still locked in a state of war. Antony and Cleopatra had escaped the carnage at Actium and fled to Alexandria, the Egyptian capital. They evidently hoped to regroup their forces and launch new attacks on Octavian's armies. Dio Cassius writes that they continued to make arrangements to carry on the war in Egypt both at sea and on land, and for this purpose they summoned all the neighboring tribes and rulers who were on friendly terms to come to their help. But they also made alternative plans, should the need arise, either to sail to Spain and stir up rebellion there, using their huge resources of money or other means, or even to shift the theater of operations to the Persian Gulf.[84]

Antony and Cleopatra, confident of victory, cavort in splendor not long before their defeat at Actium. In the weeks following the disaster, they were considerably more subdued.

Clearly, Octavian could not let the lovers go unpunished for making war on Rome. Nor could he afford to allow them to remain at large, since with Egypt's money and other resources to back them they appeared to be a potential threat to the stability of the Roman realm.

As it turned out, however, the threat Antony and Cleopatra posed to Octavian was almost nil. To the lovers' dismay, shortly after their defeat at Actium their grand dream of a new Mediterranean world quickly began to unravel. After the remains of Antony's fleet surrendered, his land troops also gave up. Without an army, he realized, he would have to recruit or hire new troops from the eastern provinces and kingdoms; and he immediately set about this task. But one by one these former allies turned against the lovers.[85] Antony and Cleopatra were now seen as pathetic losers who had no chance

The Lovers' Plans to Fight On

Even after their terrible defeat at Actium, Antony and Cleopatra held out hope that they might continue with the war and prevail over their opponent, Octavian. In this excerpt from his Roman History, *Dio Cassius summarizes some of their plans.*

"Besides the other preparations which they made for an immediate resumption of the war, Cleopatra enrolled her son Caesarion among the youths who were of an age for military service, and Antony did the same for Antyllus, who was his son by his first wife, Fulvia, and was then with him. The object of this action was to put heart into the Egyptians, who could then feel that they had a man to rule over them, and to encourage the rest of their allies to persevere [continue] in their resistance, since they would have these boys as their leaders, should any disaster overtake their parents. As far as the boys were concerned, this enrollment was to bring about their destruction. In the event Octavian spared neither, but treated them as grown men, who had been vested with some semblance of authority. As for Antony and Cleopatra, they continued to make arrangements to carry on the war in Egypt both at sea and on land, and for this purpose they summoned all the neighboring tribes and rulers who were on friendly terms to come to their aid. But they also made alternative plans, should the need arise, either to sail to Spain and stir up rebellion there, using their huge resources of money or other means, or even to shift the theater of operations to the Persian Gulf."

at all against the Roman colossus, and no one wanted to risk incurring Octavian's wrath by helping them. One local ruler was so afraid that he killed the messengers Antony sent to ask him for aid.

Making the lovers' future appear even grimmer was their realization that Octavian would soon come after them. The mood in Alexandria was fearful and somber as rulers and common people alike waited anxiously for Roman sails to appear on the horizon. That wait stretched from weeks into months as Octavian, realizing that his opponents had been abandoned by their allies, temporarily put off his advance on Egypt. During this interval, both Cleopatra and Antony sent messengers to Octavian in attempts to bribe him into sparing them. "Cleopatra promised to give him large sums of money," writes Dio, "while Antony reminded him of their friendship and of their kinship by marriage [to Octavian's sister, Octavia] . . . and he offered to take his own life if Cleopatra might be saved by this action."[86] Octavian flatly refused these desperate gestures.

A Hopeless Cause

In July 30 B.C., the long-dreaded sails of Octavian's ships finally appeared on the horizon north of Alexandria. Antony quickly marshaled his few remaining loyal troops and in the following days met Octavian's forces in some small and largely indecisive skirmishes. It was clear to all involved, however, that such diehard actions were useless and that Antony's cause was hopeless. So no one was surprised when Cleopatra's fleet and his own land

troops soon deserted him and surrendered to Octavian.[87]

With the fleet in Roman hands and Octavian's soldiers entering the city, Alexandria was in chaos. The streets were filled with panicked people, some scurrying for the imagined safety of their homes, others escaping into the desert. In the confusion, someone mistakenly told Antony that Cleopatra had been killed. According to Plutarch, he cried out in anguish, "Why delay longer, Antony? Fate has taken away the one excuse which could still make you desire to live." The defeated Roman leader then asked one of his trusted attendants to stab him. When the man refused, Antony committed the deed himself. "Then," Plutarch continues,

he stabbed himself with his own sword through the belly and fell upon the bed. But the wound did not kill him quickly. Presently, as he lay prostrate, the bleeding stopped and he came to himself and implored the bystanders to put him out of his pain. But they ran out of the room and left him writhing in agony and crying for help.[88]

Meanwhile, Cleopatra had barricaded herself, along with some servants, in her tomb, which was still under construction. Some of Antony's companions (or Cleopatra's servants; the ancient accounts differ on this point) found him and carried him, still bleeding, to the door of the tomb. Describing the heartbreaking scene that followed, Dio writes that Cleopatra

peered out over the top of the tomb. Its doors had a locking device, so that, once closed, they could not be opened again, but the upper part of the building near the roof was not yet quite completed. When some of Antony's companions saw her looking out from there, they uttered a shout which even Antony could hear, and learning that Cleopatra was still alive, he struggled to his feet as though he still had strength enough to live. But as he had lost much blood, he knew that his end was near, and implored his companions to carry him to the monument and lift him up by the ropes which had been left hanging to raise the stone blocks. This was done, and Antony died there in Cleopatra's bosom.[89]

Soon after Antony's death, Octavian's soldiers captured Cleopatra. For a few days, she remained Octavian's prisoner and made a show of offering him her money and jewels in exchange for her life. He was pleased because he wanted her to live long enough to march in chains in the triumph, or grand victory parade, he planned to stage when he returned to Rome. But as Plutarch points out, though

Shortly after Antony's suicide, Octavian meets with the imprisoned Cleopatra. Octavian's plan to march Cleopatra in chains during his victory parade was foiled when she stealthily took her own life.

Octavian felt "confident that he had deceived the queen . . . the truth was that she had deceived him."[90] The wily queen had learned of his plans to humiliate her publicly and she secretly planned her suicide. Within another few days she was dead from the bites of Egyptian asps, poisonous snakes she had pressed to her breast. On learning of the deed, Octavian, in stark contrast to his treatment of the prisoners after Philippi, did not seek vengeance on his former enemy; instead, he honored her last request to be buried beside her beloved Antony. However, he was less merciful to her son, Caesarion, who, as the last potential claimant to state power, was quietly eliminated.

Rescuing an Upside-Down Age

All of his adversaries eliminated at last, Octavian now confronted the task of reshaping the Roman government as a one-man dictatorship, an act he must have realized would change the face of the Mediterranean world forever. This act would also make him the most powerful human being who had ever lived. He apparently appreciated the enormity of this fact, for while still in Egypt he sought inspiration by visiting the tomb of Alexander the Great, another man who had faced the challenge of ruling most of the known world. That Octavian placed himself, along with Alexander, on a level far above that of ordinary kings and rulers is evident by his answer to a local man who asked him if he wanted also to visit the tombs of the Ptolemies. "I came to see the King, not a row of corpses!"[91] he loudly exclaimed.

But Octavian was considerably more subdued when he returned to Rome in August 29 B.C. A few days before the first of the three magnificent triumphs in honor of his victories, staged between August 13 and 15, he meditated in private and listened to a private reading of the *Georgics*, poems that his friend Virgil had recently written. The first poem contained a beautiful prayer that beseeched the gods to preserve the health and life of the man who promised to bring peace and order at last to a war-weary world.

> Gods of our fathers, native gods, Romulus and our mother Vesta, you who guard the Tuscan Tiber [River] and the Palatine [hill] of Rome, at least do not prevent this young man from the rescue of an age turned upside down.[92]

With this little prayer, Virgil voiced the feelings of most of his fellow Romans. The Roman Republic was dead; and memories of its failures and the turbulent, bloody events of its last decades stirred little more than emotional pain and distress in the average Roman. Sick of the seemingly endless civil discord and all the suffering and devastation it had brought, they longed for peace and harmony and believed that Octavian was the man fated to bring about a more tranquil and constructive age.

"The Great and Exalted One"

With the prayers and backing of a majority of the citizens, therefore, Octavian slowly and shrewdly consolidated a wide array of powers, always claiming to do so legally, in

This fanciful rendering of Cleopatra shows her pressing a poisonous asp to her breast. After her death, Octavian generously fulfilled her request to be buried with Antony.

accordance with Roman tradition and established law. Because of his military power, his popularity, and his apparent willingness to allow the old government to keep functioning, he won the respect of the senators. They now believed as he did that a benign dictator could bring Rome order and prosperity. So they gladly went through the fiction of legally granting him powers he either already possessed or easily could have taken by force. He was given direct control of Egypt, Gaul, and many other provinces, thus limiting the powers of the government mainly to Italy. He also

reserved the right to declare war or peace without having to consult the Senate and the right to call meetings of that body. In addition, he was granted permanent authority equal to that of the consuls and also to that of the tribunes, officials who could veto any law.[93]

This was only the beginning of the honors and powers lavished on Octavian. In a solemn ceremony on January 16, 27 B.C., the Senate thanked him for "saving the country" and bestowed upon him the name of Augustus, "the great and exalted one." This was added to the title he had

A Prince Sprung from the Gods?

Virgil was not the only Roman poet to extol Augustus's virtues during the leader's reign. Quintus Horatius Flaccus (65–8 B.C.), popularly known as Horace, became Virgil's friend and soon afterward acquired the patronage, or financial support, of Gaius Maecenas, Augustus's powerful political associate. In the following poem, titled *To Augustus*, Horace calls the ruler Rome's "Prince" and expresses the unhappiness of the Roman people when Augustus is away from the city. Such odes illustrate well how much a father figure the man formerly called Octavian had become to his war-weary and insecure subjects.

Sprung from Gods, best guard
   of Rome, long, too long,
   you leave your home.

You promised a shorter stay;
   Ah! return, the Fathers
   [Roman elders] pray.

Ah! return, your country cries,
   like the springtime to our
   skies;

Days will glide more sweetly
   o'er, suns come brighter to
   our shore.

Long they reign, good Prince,
   we pray, graced by many a
   festival day;

This our prayer at sober
   morn, this at cheerful
   evening's return.

This painting of the poet Horace captures his urbane, easygoing, and pleasant manner. Along with Virgil, Ovid, Livy, and others, he brought Roman literature to its zenith in the Augustan Age.

already assumed—*Imperator*, or "supreme commander," the term from which the word emperor later developed. Dio writes:

> At the time when [the senators and the people] wished to give him some title of special importance . . . Octavian had set his heart strongly on being named Romulus. But when he understood that this aroused suspicions that he desired the kingship [because Romulus had been Rome's first king], he abandoned his efforts to obtain it and adopted the title of Augustus, as signifying that he was something more than human, since indeed all the most precious and sacred objects are referred to as *augusta*.[94]

The people and the senators also conferred on Octavian, now known as Imperator Caesar Augustus, another special honor. According to Suetonius in *Lives of the Twelve Caesars:*

This drawing of a carved sardonyx cameo, now on display in a Vienna museum, shows Augustus and Livia (center of top panel). Note the eagle, the symbol of Rome, at their feet.

In a universal movement to confer on Augustus the title "Father of his Country," the first approach was made by the commons [members of the popular Assembly], who sent a deputation [delegation] to him. . . . When he declined this honor a huge crowd met him outside the Theater with laurel wreaths [symbols of honor and glory], and repeated the request. Finally, the Senate followed suit . . . [and] chose Valerius Messala to speak for them all. . . . Messala's words were: "Caesar Augustus, I am instructed to wish you and your family good fortune and divine blessings; which amounts to wishing that our entire State will be fortunate and our country prosperous. The Senate agrees with the people of Rome in saluting you as Father of your Country." With tears in his eyes, Augustus answered—again I quote his exact words: "Fathers of the Senate, I have at last achieved my highest ambition. What more can I ask of the immortal gods than that they may permit me to enjoy your approval until my dying day?"[95]

Through this continuous process of acquiring legal titles, honors, and powers, writes Dio, "the power both of the people and of the Senate was wholly transferred into the hands of Augustus." Dio goes on to point out that the lofty position Augustus held from then on was no different from that of a king, a title the Romans traditionally despised. "It was from this time that a monarchy, strictly speaking, was established. It would certainly be most truthful to describe it as a monarchy."[96] But Augustus was careful never to refer to himself either as king or emperor, choosing instead the title of *princeps*, meaning

An idealized portrait of Augustus and Livia. She was known for her intelligence, generosity, and modest lifestyle (their house had just twelve rooms, only five of which they regularly used).

"first citizen."[97] To further bolster his image as a simple man of the people, he and his wife Livia lived in a modest house and shunned the usual lavish lifestyle of the wealthy and powerful.

Yet in spite of Augustus's modest show, he and the rulers who succeeded him were nothing less than emperors and the huge domain they ruled became known as the Roman Empire. During the first two hundred years of imperial rule, an era later referred to as the *Pax Romana*, or "great Roman peace," the Mediterranean sphere enjoyed relative peace and unprecedented prosperity. Augustus laid the foundation for that prosperity in his forty-two-year reign, which became known as

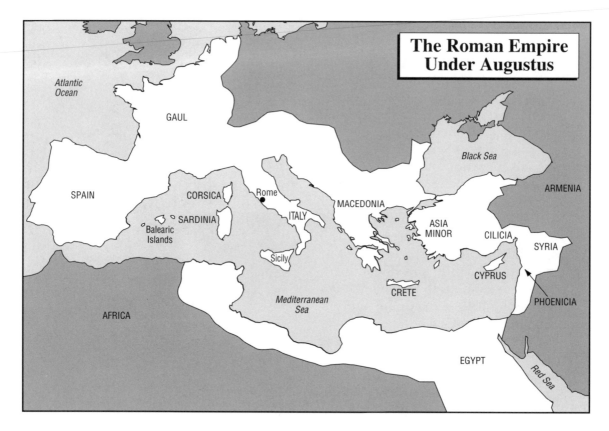

The Roman Empire Under Augustus

the Augustan Age. During these years, he kept his promise to build a firm and lasting foundation for a strong and peaceful country. He reorganized the army, created a police force for the city of Rome, reformed both the administration of the provinces and the tax system, built dozens of temples, theaters, and other public buildings, and championed the arts and literature. When he died on August 19, A.D. 14 at the age of seventy-six, millions mourned and many wept openly.

Augustus's Successors

Few of Augustus's successors ruled as well or were as widely revered and loved as he was. Some, like Caligula, Nero, and Commodus, earned lasting reputations as cruel and demented egomaniacs and tyrants. Others, including Vespasian, Trajan, Hadrian, and Antoninus Pius, were effective, constructive leaders who maintained prosperity and/or continued to expand Roman territory and authority. Under Trajan, who reigned from A.D. 98 to 117, the Empire reached its greatest extent, stretching from the Atlantic Ocean in the west to the Persian Gulf in the east, and from northern Africa in the south to central Britain in the north. In total, this huge realm encompassed some 3.5 million square miles and over 100 million people.

In time, however, the power and glory of the city and empire the Romans and many others called "immortal" faded.

Poor leadership, civil disorder, and severe economic problems increasingly weakened the Empire's military and administrative structure. At the same time, the inhabitants became disillusioned, war weary, and fearful of attacks by a growing number of external enemies.

Indeed, in the turbulent fifth century the sick and weakened Roman Empire faced its greatest challenge ever as wave after wave of invaders from western Asia and central Europe swept over its northern borders. Fierce nomadic peoples whom the Romans referred to as "barbarians"—the Goths, Huns, Vandals, Franks, and others—burned and looted Roman cities and seized former Roman lands. "The Empire was like a great whale," writes Donald Dudley, "slowed down and stopped by a school of killers, the

The emperor Trajan, during whose reign the Roman Empire reached its greatest extent. He was famous for the lavish, 123-day-long gladiatorial spectacles he staged in the Colosseum in A.D. 107.

barbarians, who were now closing in to tear it to pieces."[98] In 476, with the Empire a mere shell of its former self, the last Roman emperor, Romulus Augustulus, vacated the throne. After that, the physical and cultural decay of the old Roman administrative apparatus continued.

The Roman Legacy

Eventually, some of the small, culturally backward kingdoms that dotted the former Roman lands rose from the wreckage of the Empire and evolved into the nations of modern Europe. These states retained a rich Roman cultural legacy that included, among other things, the Latin language, concepts of law and statecraft, and classical architectural styles. Europe also inherited many stirring ancient stories, legends, and historical tracts describing the lives and deeds of the great Roman leaders who, along with leaders of other ancient nations, had shaped the course of Mediterranean civilization. Reading the accounts of Plutarch, Dio Cassius, Suetonius, and others, we can readily understand what motivated national leaders such as Sulla, Caesar, Antony, Cleopatra, and Octavian/ Augustus, whose names still loom large in the annals of Western culture. We easily recognize that the emotions that drove them—ambition, arrogance, and greed— continue to drive national leaders to acts of cruelty and aggression.

And in this comparison lies an important lesson. The events that led to the collapse of the Roman Republic were inspired by the quest for ultimate power by a few individuals. History has shown repeatedly that once a person attains such power, he or she usually misuses it, generating much misery and ruin. This is the basis for the famous adage "absolute power corrupts absolutely." Just as the Republic's representative government gave way to the Empire, with its concept of absolute one-man rule, modern democratic nations remain potential prey for the ever-present power-hungry dictator. The twentieth century, comments F. R. Cowell, saw during World War II,

> self-appointed leaders, a Duce [Italy's Benito Mussolini] and a Führer [Germany's Adolf Hitler], allowed to create and develop a private [political-military] force to such an extent that by luck, by bluff, and by extravagant combination of propaganda and intimidation, they succeeded in overawing and replacing the government of their countries. . . . We have seen how these same Nazi gangsters proceeded to apply the same tactics to their neighbors and by how narrow a margin and at what frightful cost they were withstood in order that humanity might be rescued from the rule of the jack-boot and the revolver.[99]

We Must Remain Vigilant

The rise of these and other recent dictators in various corners of the globe offers ample proof that the Sullas, Caesars, and Antonys are still with us. Those who desire to remain free of such despots must remain constantly vigilant. It is perhaps ironic that the great Cicero, whose memory, more than that of any other person, still symbolizes all that was good about the Roman Republic, so long ago recognized the importance of such vigilance. "Where the places are few and rivalry is keen," he wrote,

> the struggle often becomes so fierce that it is difficult to respect the sacred rights of society. Of this we have recently had proof in the audacity of Caesar, who overthrew all the laws of heaven and earth to gain supreme power, the object of his mad ambition. Alas! It is just the stoutest hearts, the brightest intellects, that are fired with the passion for office and command, for power and glory. Let us then be all the more watchful not to commit the like excess.[100]

Notes

Introduction: The Fall of the Republic in a Nutshell

1. Michael Crawford, *The Roman Republic.* Cambridge, MA: Harvard University Press, 1993, p. 1.

2. Chester G. Starr, *Civilization and the Caesars: The Intellectual Revolution in the Roman Empire.* New York: Norton, 1965, p. 20.

3. Starr, *Civilization and the Caesars,* pp. 17–18.

4. As will be shown, the ranks of these strongmen included one very strong woman—Cleopatra, queen of Egypt and the mistress first of Caesar and then of Antony.

5. Crawford, *The Roman Republic,* p. 2.

Chapter 1: An Appetite for War: The Growth of Roman Imperialism

6. Quoted in Garry Wills, ed., *Roman Culture: Weapons and the Man.* New York: George Braziller, 1966, p. 245.

7. Dorothy Mills, *The Book of the Ancient Romans.* New York: G. P. Putnam's Sons, 1927, p. 138.

8. Donald R. Dudley, *The Romans, 850 B.C.–A.D. 337.* New York: Knopf, 1970, p. 8.

9. Both the ancient name for the area, Etruria, and the modern, Tuscany, evolved from the name of the people—Etruscan.

10. Quoted in Michael Grant, *The World of Rome.* New York: New American Library, 1960, p. 100.

11. Virgil, *Aeneid.* Trans. Patric Dickinson. New York: New American Library, 1961, p. 14.

12. Michael Grant, *History of Rome.* New York: Scribner's, 1978, pp. 65–66.

13. Cicero, *On the Laws,* in *On the Republic and On the Laws.* Trans. Clinton W. Keyes. Cambridge, MA: Harvard University Press, 1966, pp. 375–77.

14. The inability to unite was a character flaw shared by nearly all Greek city-states in antiquity and more than any other factor brought about their collective political downfall.

15. The term *Punic* was derived from the Latin word *Punicus,* meaning Phoenician, the name of the Near Eastern seafaring people who founded Carthage in about 850 B.C.

16. Polybius, *The Histories,* vol. 1. Trans. W. R. Paton. Cambridge, MA: Harvard University Press, 1966, p. 55.

17. James Henry Breasted, *Ancient Times: A History of the Early World.* Boston: Ginn, 1944, p. 609.

18. John Warry, *Warfare in the Classical World.* Norman: University of Oklahoma Press, 1995, p. 125.

19. Naphtali Lewis, *Life in Egypt Under Roman Rule.* Oxford: Clarendon Press, 1983, p. 10.

20. Because they succeeded Alexander, they were and still are often referred to as the *Diadochi,* Greek for "Successors."

21. F. R. Cowell, *Cicero and the Roman Republic.* Baltimore: Penguin Books, 1967, pp. 209, 213.

22. A. J. Langguth, *A Noise of War: Caesar, Pompey, Octavian, and the Struggle for Rome.* New York: Simon and Schuster, 1994, pp. 29–30.

Chapter 2: Strongmen and Civil Strife: The Struggle to Maintain Order

23. In this case, "Social" derives from the Latin word *socii,* meaning "allies," since the Italian cities Rome had captured but not awarded citizenship were referred to as allies, and it was these cities that rebelled.

24. Breasted, *Ancient Times,* p. 656.

25. Lawrence Keppie, *The Making of the Roman Army: From Republic to Empire.* New York: Barnes and Noble, 1984, p. 70.

26. Plutarch, *Life of Sulla*, in *Fall of the Roman Republic: Six Lives by Plutarch*. Trans. Rex Warner. New York: Penguin Books, 1972, pp. 104–105.

27. Plutarch, *Life of Sulla*, in *Fall of the Roman Republic*, p. 105.

28. Quoted in Naphtali Lewis and Meyer Reinhold, eds., *Roman Civilization, Sourcebook I: The Republic*. New York: Harper and Row, 1966, pp. 284–85.

29. Plutarch, *Life of Crassus*, in *Fall of the Roman Republic*, p. 122.

30. The depiction of Spartacus surviving the battle and dying later by crucifixion in Howard Fast's novel *Spartacus* and in the famous film based on the book is fictitious. Both the novel and the film attempt to capture the atmosphere and pageantry of ancient Rome, however, and they are highly recommended for their moving drama and colorful portrayal of life in first-century B.C. Italy.

31. Plutarch, *Life of Crassus*, in *Fall of the Roman Republic*, p. 127.

32. Ernle Bradford, *Julius Caesar: The Pursuit of Power*. New York: Morrow, 1984, p. 81.

33. Suetonius, *Julius Caesar*, in *Lives of the Twelve Caesars*, published as *The Twelve Caesars*. Trans. Robert Graves, rev. Michael Grant. New York: Penguin Books, 1979, p. 28.

34. Suetonius, *Julius Caesar*, in *The Twelve Caesars*, pp. 50–51. The remark, "You, too, my child?"—later interpolated by Shakespeare in *Julius Caesar* as "Et tu, Brute?"—was a reference to the strong possibility that Brutus was actually Caesar's son; about the time of the younger man's birth, Caesar had been his mother's lover.

Chapter 3: A "Superb and Terrible" Struggle: The Rise of Antony and Octavian

35. Plutarch, *Life of Antony*, in *Makers of Rome: Nine Lives by Plutarch*. Trans. Ian Scott-Kilvert. New York: Penguin Books, 1965, p. 272.

36. Plutarch, *Life of Brutus*, in *Makers of Rome*, pp. 238–39.

37. Plutarch, *Life of Antony*, in *Makers of Rome*, p. 283.

38. Henry T. Rowell, *Rome in the Augustan Age*. Norman: University of Oklahoma Press, 1962, pp. 16–17.

39. Plutarch, *Life of Antony*, in *Makers of Rome*, p. 284.

40. Quoted in Rowell, *Rome in the Augustan Age*, p. 19.

41. Quoted in Michael Grant, *The Army of the Caesars*. New York: M. Evans, 1974, p. 33.

42. Quoted in Lewis and Reinhold, *Roman Civilization*, pp. 298–99.

43. John B. Firth, *Augustus Caesar and the Organization of the Empire of Rome*. Freeport, NY: Books for the Libraries Press, 1972, pp. 77–78.

44. Plutarch, *Life of Cicero*, in *Fall of the Roman Republic*, pp. 359–60.

45. In a detailed discourse on the triumvirs' proscriptions in his *Roman History*, Appian also describes Cicero's demise. According to Appian, Antony kept Cicero's head propped up on his dinner table until he could no longer stomach the sight of it.

46. Appian, *Roman History*. Trans. Horace White. Cambridge, MA: Harvard University Press, 1964, p. 353.

47. Quoted in Rowell, *Rome in the Augustan Age*, p. 31.

48. Suetonius, *Augustus*, in *The Twelve Caesars*, pp. 59–60.

Chapter 4: Prophecies and Propaganda: The World Divided into Opposing Camps

49. Egypt was a particularly important asset. Though militarily weak, it boasted considerable resources of grain and other commodities; and its queen, Cleopatra, possessed great wealth. Her unique political situation was that

she had borne Julius Caesar a son, Caesarion, who was six at the time of the battles at Philippi. It was not lost on Octavian and Antony that the boy, as another of Caesar's heirs, might eventually have a role to play in the struggle for power.

50. Rowell, *Rome in the Augustan Age*, p. 35.

51. Plutarch, *Life of Antony*, in *Lives of the Noble Grecians and Romans*. Trans. John Dryden. New York: Random House, 1932, p. 1,119.

52. Plutarch, *Life of Antony*, in *Makers of Rome*, p. 288.

53. Plutarch, *Life of Antony*, in *Lives*, pp. 1,118–19.

54. Plutarch, *Life of Antony*, in *Lives*, p. 1,119.

55. Peter Green, *Alexander to Actium: The Historical Evolution of the Hellenistic Age*. Berkeley and Los Angeles: University of California Press, 1990, p. 672.

56. Appian, *Roman History*, p. 389.

57. Antony's choice of Cleopatra over Octavia was undoubtedly motivated in large degree by the knowledge that Octavian was preparing a power play against him in Italy; Cleopatra had the renowned treasure of the Ptolemies, with which Antony could do much to counter this threat.

58. Firth, *Augustus Caesar*, p. 136.

59. Dudley, *The Romans*, p. 141.

60. Firth, *Augustus Caesar*, p. 138.

61. Dio Cassius, *Roman History*. Trans. Ian Scott-Kilvert. New York: Penguin Books, 1987, pp. 38–39.

62. Plutarch, *Life of Antony*, in *Lives*, p. 1,135.

63. Dio Cassius, *Roman History*, p. 38.

64. Quoted in Jack Lindsay, *Cleopatra*. London: Constable, 1970, p. 202.

65. Antony and Cleopatra also moved these peoples by the announcement of their intention to unite the Ptolemaic and Seleucid kingdoms and raise them to their former glories; Antony's minting of Roman coins bearing his and Cleopatra's images; and Cleopatra's new and ominous public slogan, "As surely as I shall yet dispense justice on the Roman Capitol [Capitoline Hill]."

Chapter 5: The Victor's Wrath and the People's Justice: The Battle of Actium

66. Plutarch, *Life of Antony*, in *Makers of Rome*, p. 324.

67. Plutarch, *Life of Antony*, in *Makers of Rome*, p. 324.

68. W. L. Rodgers, *Greek and Roman Naval Warfare*. Annapolis: Naval Institute Press, 1964, p. 529.

69. Rodgers, *Greek and Roman Naval Warfare*, p. 530.

70. Plutarch, *Life of Antony*, in *Lives*, p. 1,138.

71. Plutarch, *Life of Antony*, in *Makers of Rome*, p. 329.

72. Plutarch, *Life of Antony*, in *Lives*, p. 1,141.

73. Dio Cassius, *Roman History*, pp. 47, 50.

74. Dio Cassius, *Roman History*, pp. 52–53, 55.

75. Dio Cassius, *Roman History*, pp. 57–58.

76. Dio Cassius, *Roman History*, p. 59.

77. Plutarch, *Life of Antony*, in *Lives*, p. 1,141.

78. Plutarch, *Life of Antony*, in *Makers of Rome*, p. 332.

79. Plutarch, *Life of Antony*, in *Lives*, p. 1,142.

80. Ernle Bradford, *Cleopatra*. New York: Harcourt Brace Jovanovich, 1972, p. 237.

81. Dio Cassius, *Roman History*, p. 60.

82. Dio Cassius, *Roman History*, p. 61.

Chapter 6: Republic Gives Way to Empire: The Lesson of Absolute Power

83. Quoted in Dudley, *The Romans*, p. 116.

84. Dio Cassius, *Roman History*, pp. 67–68.

85. One of those who switched allegiance to Octavian was Herod the Great, Rome's vassal king of Judaea, in Palestine, who took with

him several legions that Antony sorely needed.

86. Dio Cassius, *Roman History*, p. 69.

87. Plutarch writes (in *Life of Antony*) that after one skirmish Antony brought to the palace a soldier who had fought particularly valiantly for him. There Cleopatra rewarded the man with a gold breastplate and helmet. Ironically, that very night the soldier deserted them for Octavian.

88. Plutarch, *Life of Antony*, in *Makers of Rome*, p. 341.

89. Dio Cassius, *Roman History*, pp. 71–72.

90. Plutarch, *Life of Antony*, in *Makers of Rome*, p. 346.

91. Quoted in Dio Cassius, *Roman History*, p. 77.

92. Quoted in Dudley, *The Romans*, p. 139.

93. By tradition, tribunes could also preside over the people's Assembly, defend citizens' rights, and arrest corrupt officials, even consuls. Thus, with the tribunician authority, Octavian gained special and wide-ranging powers over both groups and individuals.

94. Dio Cassius, *Roman History*, p. 140.

95. Suetonius, *Augustus*, in *The Twelve Caesars*, p. 87.

96. Dio Cassius, *Roman History*, p. 140.

97. From this word came the term *Principate*, denoting Augustus's long reign and the imperial government structure he created.

98. Donald R. Dudley, *The Civilization of Rome*. New York: New American Library, 1960, p. 219.

99. Cowell, *Cicero and the Roman Republic*, p. 376.

100. Cicero, *On Moral Duties*, in *The Basic Works of Cicero*. Ed. Moses Hadas, trans. George B. Gardiner. New York: Random House, 1951, p. 13.

For Further Reading

Lionel Casson, *Daily Life in Ancient Rome.* New York: American Heritage Publishing, 1975. A well-written presentation by a highly respected scholar of how the Romans lived: their homes, streets, entertainments, eating habits, theaters, religion, slaves, marriage customs, tombstone epitaphs, and more.

———, *Daily Life in Ancient Egypt.* New York: American Heritage Publishing, 1975. Another excellent presentation by Casson, this one about life and customs in Egypt, which Cleopatra ruled during the final years of the doomed Roman Republic.

Peter Connolly, *Greece and Rome at War.* London: Macdonald, 1981. A highly informative and useful volume by one of the finest historians of ancient military affairs. Connolly, whose stunning paintings adorn this and his other books, is also the foremost modern illustrator of the ancient world. Highly recommended.

Anthony Marks and Graham Tingay, *The Romans.* London: Usborne, 1990. A beautifully illustrated summary of Roman history and most aspects of daily life, presented for basic readers.

Don Nardo, *The Roman Republic; The Roman Empire;* and *Cleopatra.* All: San Diego: Lucent Books, 1994; *Julius Caesar, The Age of Augustus, Caesar's Conquest of Gaul,* and *Life in Ancient Rome.* All: San Diego: Lucent Books, 1996; *Greek and Roman Mythology.* San Diego: Lucent Books, 1997; *The Fall of the Roman Empire* and *Life as a Roman Slave.* Both: San Diego: Lucent Books, forthcoming. These comprehensive but easy-to-read overviews of various aspects of Roman civilization provide a broader context for understanding the leaders, trends, ideas, themes, and events surrounding the devastating Roman civil wars of the first century B.C., the subsequent fall of the Republic, and its replacement by the Empire.

Martha Rofheart, *The Alexandrian.* New York: Thomas Y. Crowell, 1976. A colorful historical novel about the legendary queen Cleopatra, blending evidence from ancient sources, such as Plutarch and Appian, with fictional situations and details.

Chester G. Starr, *The Ancient Romans.* New York: Oxford University Press, 1971. A commendable basic survey of Roman history, with several interesting sidebars on such subjects as the Etruscans, Roman law, and the Roman army. Also contains many primary source quotations by ancient Greek and Roman writers.

Major Works Consulted

Ancient Sources

Appian, *Roman History*. Trans. Horace White. Cambridge, MA: Harvard University Press, 1964. Appian, an Alexandrian Greek who became a Roman citizen, wrote a history of Rome from about 135 to 35 B.C., covering in some detail the fateful civil wars that sounded the death knell of the Republic.

Julius Caesar, *Commentaries on the Gallic War* and *Civil Wars*, published as *War Commentaries of Caesar*. Trans. Rex Warner. New York: New American Library, 1960. Caesar, as gifted a writer as he was a general and politician, left behind these fabulously detailed accounts of his personal battlefield and campaign experiences, affording us a fascinating glimpse into the mind of one of the greatest military leaders who ever lived.

Cicero, *Letters to Atticus*. 3 vols. Trans. E. O. Winstedt. Cambridge, MA: Harvard University Press, 1961; *Selected Political Speeches of Cicero*. Trans. Michael Grant. Baltimore: Penguin Books, 1979; *The Basic Works of Cicero*. Ed. Moses Hadas, trans. George B. Gardiner. New York: Random House, 1951; and *On the Republic and On the Laws*. Trans. Clinton W. Keyes. Cambridge, MA: Harvard University Press, 1966. Cicero's letters, speeches, and essays contain a wealth of information about political leaders and events during the first century B.C., as well as the attitudes and viewpoints of the Roman upper classes of the time.

Dio Cassius, *Roman History*. Trans. Ian Scott-Kilvert. New York: Penguin Books, 1987. An excellent translation of Dio's important work about the events of Augustus Caesar's (Octavian's) rise to power and reign as the first Roman emperor.

Naphtali Lewis and Meyer Reinhold, eds., *Roman Civilization, Sourcebook I: The Republic*. New York: Harper and Row, 1966. A massive and very useful compendium of English translations of hundreds of surviving Greek and Roman documents and writings from Rome's republican years. Includes passages by Plutarch, Pliny, Ovid, Livy, Cicero, Suetonius, Sallust, Appian, and many others, as well as inscriptions, government documents, decrees, public laws, letters, and so on.

Plutarch, *Lives of the Noble Grecians and Romans*. Trans. John Dryden. New York: Random House, 1932; also excerpted in *Fall of the Roman Republic: Six Lives by Plutarch*. Trans. Rex Warner. New York: Penguin Books, 1972; and *Makers of Rome: Nine Lives by Plutarch*. Trans. Ian Scott-Kilvert. New York: Penguin Books, 1965. We are indebted to Plutarch, a Greek who lived and wrote in the late first and early second centuries A.D., for his biographies of ancient Greek and Roman figures, which contain much valuable information that would otherwise be lost. His lives of Antony and Caesar both contain extensive passages about Cleopatra, as well as information and anecdotes about the civil wars, triumvirates, Battle of Actium, and disintegration of the Republic. For related material, I also refer to the lives of Marius, Sulla, Pompey, Crassus, Cicero, and Brutus.

Polybius, *The Histories*, vol. 1. Trans. W. R. Paton. Cambridge, MA: Harvard University Press, 1966. This Greek historian's works are valuable for their often detailed coverage of the wars the Romans fought against Carthage and the Greek kingdoms of the eastern Mediterranean during the third and second centuries B.C.

William G. Sinnegin, ed., *Sources in Western Civilization: Rome*. New York: Free Press, 1965. A fine selection of Greek and Roman writings, including excerpts from works by Livy, Polybius, Appian, Cicero, Suetonius, and others. Also contains the *Res gestae*, the short but important work written by Augustus (Octavian).

Suetonius, *Lives of the Twelve Caesars*, published as *The Twelve Caesars*. Trans. Robert Graves, rev. Michael Grant. New York: Penguin Books, 1979. Suetonius's biographies of Caesar and Augustus contain much valuable information relating to the civil wars and collapse of the Republic.

Tacitus, *The Annals*, published as *The Annals of Imperial Rome*. Trans. Michael Grant. New York: Penguin Books, 1989. An excellent translation of Tacitus, the premier historian of the early Roman Empire, whom Thomas Jefferson referred to as "the first [foremost] writer in the world." This was barely an exaggeration, for Tacitus possessed superb narrative skill and profound insight into human nature; and the result is riveting reading that is also largely reliable history.

Virgil, *Aeneid*. Trans. Patric Dickinson. New York: New American Library, 1961. The sublime epic poet of antiquity after the Greek Homer, Virgil embodied the vigorous and, in modern terms, arrogant spirit of Roman superiority over other peoples. His works promoted the idea that the march of Rome toward a higher civilization was the most significant movement in human history.

Modern Sources

E. Badian, *Roman Imperialism in the Late Republic*. Ithaca, NY: Cornell University Press, 1968. A scholarly work that examines Roman partisan politics, greed, and the drive for foreign expansion in the Republic's last two and most turbulent centuries.

F. R. Cowell, *Cicero and the Roman Republic*. Baltimore: Penguin Books, 1967. A very detailed and insightful analysis of the late Republic, its leaders, and the problems that led to its collapse. Very highly recommended.

Michael Crawford, *The Roman Republic*. Cambridge, MA: Harvard University Press, 1993. This study of the Republic offers various insights into the political, cultural, and intellectual forces that drove the engines of change and led eventually to the death of republicanism and rise of the Principate.

John B. Firth, *Augustus Caesar and the Organization of the Empire of Rome*. Freeport, NY: Books for the Libraries Press, 1972. Beginning with Caesar's assassination in 44 B.C., this is a detailed, thoughtful telling of the final years of the Republic, including Octavian's rise to power during the civil wars and his ascendancy as Augustus, the first Roman emperor.

Michael Grant, *Caesar*. London: Weidenfeld and Nicolson, 1974. A fine biography by one of the most respected and prolific of classical historians.

———, *History of Rome*. New York: Scribner's, 1978. Like Grant's other volumes on Roman civilization, this study is comprehensive, insightful, and well written; it provides a very clear understanding of the problems that led to the fall of the Republic.

Sir John Hackett, ed., *Warfare in the Ancient World*. New York: Facts On File, 1989. An excellent analysis of the weapons, siege devices, and military customs and strategies of the major ancient cultures. Each culture is covered by a world-class historian; for this volume on the fall of the Republic, I consulted especially the essays: "The Roman Army of the Age of Polybius," by Peter Connolly (who also illustrated Hackett's book), and "The Roman Army of the Later Republic," by Lawrence Keppie (author of *The Making of the Roman Army: From Republic to Empire;* see Additional Works Consulted).

A. J. Langguth, *A Noise of War: Caesar, Pompey, Octavian, and the Struggle for Rome*. New York: Simon and Schuster, 1994. A lively, entertaining, and detailed account of the civil wars, political intrigues, and vaunting personal ambitions that marked the downfall of the Roman Republic.

Additional Works Consulted

Lesley Adkins and Roy A. Adkins, *Handbook to Life in Ancient Rome.* New York: Facts On File, 1994.

Mary Beard and Michael Crawford, *Rome in the Late Republic: Problems and Interpretations.* London: Duckworth, 1985.

Ernle Bradford, *Cleopatra.* New York: Harcourt Brace Jovanovich, 1972.

————, *Julius Caesar: The Pursuit of Power.* New York: Morrow, 1984.

James Henry Breasted, *Ancient Times: A History of the Early World.* Boston: Ginn, 1944.

John Buchan, *Augustus.* London: Hodder and Stoughton, 1937.

R. H. Burrow, *The Romans.* Baltimore: Penguin Books, 1949.

Tim Cornell and John Matthews, *Atlas of the Roman World.* New York: Facts On File, 1982.

Donald R. Dudley, *The Civilization of Rome.* New York: New American Library, 1960.

————, *The Romans, 850 B.C.–A.D. 337.* New York: Knopf, 1970.

Michael Grant, *The World of Rome.* New York: New American Library, 1960.

————, *The Army of the Caesars.* New York: M. Evans, 1974.

————, *The Founders of the Western World: A History of Greece and Rome.* New York: Scribner's, 1991.

————, *Atlas of Classical History.* New York: Oxford University Press, 1994.

————, *Greek and Roman Historians: Information and Misinformation.* London: Routledge, 1995.

Peter Green, *Alexander to Actium: The Historical Evolution of the Hellenistic Age.* Berkeley and Los Angeles: University of California Press, 1990.

Kevin Guinagh and Alfred P. Dorjahn, eds., *Latin Literature in Translation.* New York: Longman's, Green, 1952.

W. G. Hardy, *The Greek and Roman World.* Cambridge, MA: Schenkman Publishing, 1960.

Elenor G. Huzar, *Mark Antony: A Biography.* Minneapolis: University of Minnesota Press, 1978.

Archer Jones, *The Art of War in the Western World.* New York: Oxford University Press, 1987.

Anthony Kamm, *The Romans: An Introduction.* London: Routledge, 1995.

John Keegan, *A History of Warfare.* New York: Random House, 1993.

Lawrence Keppie, *The Making of the Roman Army: From Republic to Empire.* New York: Barnes and Noble, 1984.

Phillip A. Kildahl, *Caius Marius.* New York: Twayne Publishing, 1968.

Naphtali Lewis, *Life in Egypt Under Roman Rule.* Oxford: Clarendon Press, 1983.

Jack Lindsay, *Cleopatra.* London: Constable, 1970.

Dorothy Mills, *The Book of the Ancient Romans.* New York: G. P. Putnam's Sons, 1927.

Thomas N. Mitchell, *Cicero: The Senior Statesman.* New Haven, CT: Yale University Press, 1991.

W. L. Rodgers, *Greek and Roman Naval Warfare*. Annapolis: Naval Institute Press, 1964.

Henry T. Rowell, *Rome in the Augustan Age*. Norman: University of Oklahoma Press, 1962.

Chris Scarre, *Historical Atlas of Ancient Rome*. New York: Penguin Books, 1995.

Chester G. Starr, *Civilization and the Caesars: The Intellectual Revolution in the Roman Empire*. New York: Norton, 1965.

————, *A History of the Ancient World*. New York: Oxford University Press, 1991.

Lily Ross Taylor, *Party Politics in the Age of Caesar*. Berkeley and Los Angeles: University of California Press, 1968.

John Warry, *Warfare in the Classical World*. Norman: University of Oklahoma Press, 1995.

Garry Wills, ed., *Roman Culture: Weapons and the Man*. New York: George Braziller, 1966.

Index

Picture Credits

Cover photo: Giraudon/Art Resource, NY

Archive Photos, 62, 69, 73, 88, 89

Copyright British Museum, 93

Corbis-Bettmann, 36, 44, 57, 86

Library of Congress, 32, 40, 52, 67

North Wind Picture Archives, 11, 16, 21, 22, 24, 26, 29, 30, 33, 39, 46, 59, 61, 64, 70, 80, 90, 91

Stock Montage, Inc., 12, 15, 18, 51, 76, 83

About the Author

Classical historian and award-winning writer Don Nardo has published more than twenty books about the ancient Greek and Roman world. These include general histories, such as *The Roman Empire, The Persian Empire,* and *Philip and Alexander: The Unification of Greece;* war chronicles, such as *The Punic Wars* and *The Battle of Marathon;* cultural studies, such as *Life in Ancient Greece, Greek and Roman Theater,* and *The Trial of Socrates;* and literary companions to the works of Homer and Sophocles. His books about Julius Caesar, Cleopatra, the Roman Republic, and the Age of Augustus can be considered companion volumes to this one on the collapse of the Republic. Mr. Nardo also writes screenplays and teleplays and composes music. He lives with his wife, Christine, and dog, Bud, on Cape Cod, Massachusetts.